STUDIES

IN THE

SOCIAL ASPECTS

OF THE

DEPRESSION

Studies in the Social Aspects of the Depression

Advisory Editor: *ALEX BASKIN*

State University of New York at Stony Brook

RESEARCH MEMORANDUM ON SOCIAL ASPECTS OF CONSUMPTION IN THE DEPRESSION

By ROLAND S. VAILE

ARNO PRESS

A NEW YORK TIMES COMPANY

Reprint Edition 1972 by Arno Press Inc.

Reprinted from a copy in The Newark Public Library

LC# 79-162845
ISBN 0-405-00848-1

Studies in the Social Aspects of the Depression
ISBN for complete set: 0-405-00840-6
See last pages of this volume for titles.

Manufactured in the United States of America

Preface to the New Edition

In the Fall of 1930, the International Apple Shippers Association, faced with the prospect of a substantial surplus, conceived the brilliant idea of selling its product on credit at wholesale prices to the unemployed. Within weeks, 6000 men and women were hawking their wares on New York City streets. Other municipalities reported similar scenes. The success of the venture was clear: By mid-November the surplus had been consumed and prices rose from $1.75 to $2.25 per crate.

The joy which was felt by apple producers was not known universally through the land. The expanding number of unemployed grew more cautious and more prudent with the passing of each unreplenished coin. Storekeepers were asked and, in many cases, volunteered to carry known customers on the tab until some funds could be mustered with which to pay the outstanding bill. Idle men often clustered into tight little groups to discuss, argue and debate the causes and cures of the Depression. The words "overproduction" and "underconsumption" were in vogue and few conversations of the current scene passed without their mention.

In this book, the subject of Mr. Vaile's study is consumption. He has taken one of the most delicate of the numerous concerns which has faced the consumer during periods of cyclical fluctuation and described the attendant problems. He has explored the relationship between purchasing power and productivity and singled out those areas where information was lacking and where further research was necessary. The crisis which confronted small businessmen decades ago concerns small businessmen today. The pattern toward bigness which gained momentum in the 1930's has not waned in the 1970's. It seems to gain strength daily.

The issue of consumer protection—a major concern following the revelations in Upton Sinclair's 1906 muckraking novel, *The Jungle*—has again risen in the American consciousness after a period of extended hibernation. Public and private agencies now issue warnings of dangers which menace the health and welfare of the unsuspecting buyer. Ralph Nader has emerged as a folk-hero who has focused the public eye and mind on the misdeeds and complete abandon of some of the nations most eminent and wealthy corporations. The power of the consumer looms large on the horizon. At present, as in the 1930's, it is unharnessed and undirected. Viewed optimistically, we can only see consumer power as a potential force whose time has not yet come.

Alex Baskin
Stony Brook, New York, 1971

BULLETIN 35

1937

RESEARCH MEMORANDUM ON SOCIAL ASPECTS OF CONSUMPTION IN THE DEPRESSION

By ROLAND S. VAILE

Professor of Marketing
University of Minnesota

With the Assistance of HELEN G. CANOYER

PREPARED UNDER THE DIRECTION OF THE
COMMITTEE ON STUDIES IN SOCIAL
ASPECTS OF THE DEPRESSION

SOCIAL SCIENCE RESEARCH COUNCIL
230 PARK AVENUE   NEW YORK NY

The Social Science Research Council was organized in 1923 and formally incorporated in 1924. composed of representatives chosen from the seven constituent societies and from time to time from related disciplines such as law, geography, psychiatry, medicine, and others. It is the purpose of the Council to plan, foster, promote, and develop research in the social field.

CONSTITUENT ORGANIZATIONS

American Anthropological Association

American Economic Association

American Historical Association

American Political Science Association

American Psychological Association

American Sociological Society

American Statistical Association

FOREWORD

By the Committee on Studies in
Social Aspects of the Depression

THIS monograph on research pertaining to social aspects of consumption in the depression is one of a series of thirteen sponsored by the Social Science Research Council to stimulate the study of depression effects on various social institutions. The full list of titles is on page ii.

The depression of the early 1930's was like the explosion of a bomb dropped in the midst of society. All the major social institutions, such as the government, family, church, and school, obviously were profoundly affected and the repercussions were so far reaching that scarcely any type of human activity was untouched. The facts about the impact of the depression on social life, however, have been only partially recorded. It would be valuable to have assembled the vast record of influence of this economic depression on society. Such a record would constitute an especially important preparation for meeting the shock of the next depression, if and when it comes. Theories must be discussed and explored now, if much of the information to test them is not to be lost amid ephemeral sources.

The field is so broad that selection has been necessary. In keeping with its mandate from the Social Science Research Council, the Committee sponsored no studies of an exclusively economic or political nature. The subjects chosen for inclusion were limited in number by resources. The final selection was made by the Committee from a larger number of proposed subjects, on the basis of social importance and available personnel.

v

Although the monographs clearly reveal a uniformity of goal, they differ in the manner in which the various authors sought to attain that goal. This is a consequence of the Committee's belief that the promotion of research could best be served by not imposing rigid restrictions on the organization of materials by the contributors. It is felt that the encouraged freedom in approach and organization has resulted in the enrichment of the individual reports and of the series as a whole.

A common goal without rigidity in procedure was secured by requesting each author to examine critically the literature on the depression for the purpose of locating existing data and interpretations already reasonably well established, of discovering the more serious inadequacies in information, and of formulating research problems feasible for study. He was not expected to do this research himself. Nor was he expected to compile a full and systematically treated record of the depression as experienced in his field. Nevertheless, in indicating the new research which is needed, the writers found it necessary to report to some extent on what is known. These volumes actually contain much information on the social influences of the depression, in addition to their analyses of pressing research questions.

The undertaking was under the staff direction of Dr. Samuel A. Stouffer, who worked under the restrictions of a short time limit in order that prompt publication might be assured. He was assisted by Mr. Philip M. Hauser and Mr. A. J. Jaffe. The Committee wishes to express appreciation to the authors, who contributed their time and effort without remuneration, and to the many other individuals who generously lent aid and materials.

William F. Ogburn Chairman
Shelby M. Harrison
Malcolm M. Willey

CONTENTS

Chapter I

Introduction

As ONE of the series of monographs on the social aspects of cyclical fluctuations, with emphasis on the period 1929-36, this volume occupies a somewhat special position.

Very narrowly conceived, research on consumption might be considered the special province of the economist, and, therefore, rather beyond the scope of the present series, which seeks to focus on sociological problems. Very broadly conceived, research on consumption might be thought to embrace the whole field of social life, since many of the underlying problems of the family, of health, of education, of recreation, of reading, or, indeed, of crime, are problems of consumption. But these fields and others as well are treated independently in separate monographs in the present series.

PURPOSE AND SCOPE

The point of view of this monograph tends to the broader, rather than the narrower, concept of consumption as a field of research. It seeks to provide a background and perspective which will supplement the work of other authors in this series, with the minimum of overlapping. Necessarily, a considerable proportion of this volume is occupied with some of the basic problems which have been traditionally the concern of the economist. There are, for example, research problems of a fundamental character associated with the measurement of income, retail trade, family expenditures, savings, and credit. Attention is given to the sources of information on these subjects and to ways and means by which the measurement of these factors in the depression might be improved. Sociologists who study the underlying influence of changes in consumption in their special domains of interest must reckon with the imperfections of these basic sources of economic information. In treating the social implications themselves, this monograph seeks to be concise and illustrative, rather than comprehensive.

The objective is the promotion and stimulation of research. The method is to raise questions, review typical data bearing on these questions, point out gaps and imperfections, and suggest points at which new research is needed.

SOME QUESTIONS AND ATTITUDES

During the cyclical movements of the 1930's there have been profound changes in both industrial and individual life. In many cases it is impossible to assign definite causes to these changes. Some of them are the result of long-time movements with which the depression did not seriously interfere, while others were caused by or materially accelerated by the depression.

There are certain broad questions which may be asked about any of the phenomena associated with consumption in the depression. For example:

1. What happened during the period?
2. Why did these things occur?
3. How much of what has happened may be considered advantageous and how much disadvantageous, and to whom have the effects accrued?
4. How, if at all, may the advantageous movements be increased and the disadvantageous ones eliminated or reduced in the future?

The third question is normative. It may not be of itself an object of scientific study. But it provides, in combination with the fourth question, the ultimate motivation for studies of the type considered in this monograph. It is first necessary to know what happened, and, accordingly, this monograph will deal largely with the first question.

Many years ago Adam Smith pointed out that "consumption

is the sole end and purpose of all production; and the interest of the producer ought to be attended to only so far as it may be necessary for promoting that of the consumer." To the extent that this is true, studies of the depression must finally be referred to the effect on the consumer. Clearly production has been and must remain merely a means to an end; it is not an end in itself. If one may speak in slogans: "The consumer is King. Long live the King!"

The attitude expressed in the preceding paragraph may be justified only with a very broad definition of consumption. In such a definition the total satisfaction that individuals get out of life must be considered as the total of consumption. This includes, of course, the satisfaction one gets out of work and play as well as that which comes with the use of material goods.

No statistical study can measure total consumption as just defined, for we have no unit of measurement for total satisfactions. Perhaps there is no best way of limiting the definition. Practically, it is possible, however, to make some approach through a study of those portions of consumption for which objective information is available.

It must be made clear at the outset that there are at least three aspects of each of the questions that have been asked above. These may be spoken of as the economic, the psychological, and the sociological implications of each occurrence. The first deals with efficiency in the production and distribution of material income; the second deals with changing personal responses to economic and social situations; the third deals with the effects on groups and on social institutions. Consequently, it follows that the effect of cyclical movements on individuals has come in part through the direct effect on industry, in part through the indirect effect on the psychology of the individual, and in part through changes in social organization and ethical evaluations.

As industry has passed through the various phases of the business cycle, income has changed, both in total quantity and in distribution. This has been accompanied by changes in individual purchasing power and, consequently, in consumption patterns. Statistical measurement of these changes in income and consumption are inadequate, however, to show the full effect. Perhaps the history of the cellophane industry may be used to illustrate some of the different effects. It may be that the developments in this particular industry were not caused directly by the depression, but they were coincident with it and have the same sort of repercussion as though a direct result of general cyclical movements. The case may be briefed as follows: When the affiliated DuPont interests found their industrial market for various products reduced, they searched diligently for something that would maintain in part their volume of sales; the sales manager for cellophane was urged to undertake an elaborate campaign for the expansion of sales; cellophane appeared during the early part of the depression in many new places. The success with which sales of this material were increased had its direct effect on employment and distribution of income within the industry itself; employees of this particular company were able to continue their accustomed standard of living and to avoid relief more effectively than could the employees in many other lines. The consumption by these particular employees is included in the indexes of retail sales, but the new activity in the industry had other effects as well. People not directly engaged in the industry came to have a new point of view concerning the packaging of merchandise; they put a new emphasis on cleanliness and freshness of commodities; they were led to purchase more by eye than previously. No study of the effects of the depression on the consumer can be complete unless it includes consideration of such derivative or indirect effects.

Differences between Depressions

Even if reasonably complete information could be gathered on the various points that need measurement, the fact must be kept in mind that no two depressions are alike. The duration and severity of depressions differ. The timing of the various phenomena of cyclical change is never twice precisely the same. The attack made on the depression difficulties is different under one administration or in one generation than in another. The cultural heritage and traditions of the people both individually and in the social organizations differ with the passage of years. In search of relief from certain features of the depression of the 1870's, many people moved westward and definitely accepted a lower physical standard of living as they dug themselves into sod huts on the prairie. They maintained, however, a relatively high degree of individual initiative. In contrast, during the depression of the 1930's social agencies, many of them highly paternalistic, furnished the main source of relief. It seems possible that, by and large, there was less reduction in the immediate standard of living of the masses in the 1930's than in the 1870's. It seems equally clear, however, that there was a greater departure from individual self-reliance, the full effect of which cannot be measured for another generation.

Methods of Reporting Changes

One of the easy ways of reporting apparent changes in well-being is through the use of data on money income. Some of the shortcomings of this method are obvious and well understood. For example, the purchasing power of the dollar is continuously changing. Moreover, it is difficult to determine what portion of money income is used for immediate consumption and what part is reserved for future consumption. Still further and perhaps more baffling is the question of what part of the individual monetary expenditures is used for the direct attainment of satisfactions and what part is used to pave the way in some necessary detail for the attainment of specific satisfactions.

Another estimate of the change in consumption can be made by noting the expenditure for physical goods. Such measurement contains the difficulty already referred to, that price levels and purchasing power of money are continuously shifting. Some estimate of this shift can be measured and removed from the expenditure data by the use of price indexes. These are, at best, imperfect devices, and one of the needs for further study and administrative action is in the preparation of more adequate price indexes for various specific purposes.

In some cases production data may be used to check against the data on expenditure for consumption. In using this sort of information care must be taken to allow properly for international and inter-regional trade. The difficulties of monetary measurement are present here, except in those cases where data on physical units produced are available. Even in these cases, changes in quality of goods may mask true changes in quantity.

In the use of data on either expenditure for or production of physical goods, care must be taken to differentiate between immediate consumption goods, deferred consumption goods, and production goods. Each of these is important but in different ways and the implications of each must be distinguished clearly.

Numerous attempts have been made to measure monetary income in the United States. Data also have been collected, analyzed, and adjusted into estimates of real income. Some of the studies deal mainly with national totals. Others show frequency distributions of individual incomes under various classifications such as size of income, its source, the occupations of the individuals, and so on. No one of the estimates is perfect in scope and accuracy; in fact, all of them together leave much to be desired. Perhaps this is inherent in the problem, but continuing effort should bring a degree of improvement in the basic data available for analysis. Some consideration of the shortcomings of present information in income is undertaken in Chapter II of this memorandum. These shortcomings suggest problems for investigation of statistical reporting that do not bear on the depression alone, but without which depression effects cannot be adequately interpreted.

Non-Monetary Income and Consumption

However carefully the data on physical goods may be gathered, manipulated, and interpreted there remains a problem of equal importance and greater difficulty. It is necessary to estimate the part that consumption of physical goods plays in total satisfactions. This part must be compared against that furnished by work, play, "high thinking and simple living," services of all sorts, the entire category of leisure, and other more or less intangible sorts of satisfactions. This is not a simple task. It involves ethical or other valuations of non-monetary phenomena. The greatest difficulty lies, perhaps, in the fact that there are few recorded data.

Perhaps the largest single element of error in the monetary measure of individual income is the varying proportion of activities or consumption that do not enter into market transactions. For example, the services of the housewife nowhere show in the monetary income. It is perhaps an open question whether the redirection in monetary expenditure that appears when a family decides to carry on without a maid truly measures a reduction in satisfactions. Certainly, there is a change in activity on the part of certain members of the household, but it may be that food is better prepared, and there is less of irritation due to the servant problem. Certainly a change from eating at a restaurant, where the preparation of the food does appear in the monetary transactions, to eating at home may result in improved health.

Among the other intangibles—or perhaps we should say imponderables—none is more deserving of attention than the differences in personal and social effects produced by activities carried out by individual initiative, on the one hand, and those that result from a socially planned program of consumption, on the other. The contrast between Works Progress Administration projects and the informal work "bees" of a generation or two ago is interesting, both in respect to the spontaneity with which projects are undertaken and in respect to the spirit in which they are completed. No study of the effect of the depression on the consumer is complete unless it includes an evaluation of the change in attitude of the people toward a community tennis court, for example, when it has been built (a) spontaneously after formal working hours by those who will use it (b) by an established government agency from funds appropriated specifically for the purpose, or (c) by a group of relief workers as a "make work" undertaking. Perhaps "rational" people would make no distinction based on the source of the paraphernalia from which their satisfactions come, but there is a school of psychologists which claims that satisfactions are related closely to the efforts necessary for their attainment.

While changes in money income are important, still no study of the effect of the depression is complete that does not pay some attention to these non-monetary phenomena.

GOVERNMENTAL AND GROUP ACTIVITIES

It is obvious to the casual observer that the depression has brought important changes in the part played by government. These changes have included various experiments in production control, in the re-distribution of income through taxation and other measures, in the selection and care of the wards of the state, and in the new emphasis on government-directed activities that are very close to direct consumption. Among the latter may be included the development of park systems by various units of government and the emphasis on recreation not only in these park areas but elsewhere. Each of these shifts in government activity has resulted, necessarily, in some change in consumption. Production control in agriculture was designed to increase the farm prices of certain commodities. Any success of this objective was accompanied by an increase in the consumer price of these commodities relative to others. This change in relative prices resulted in a new pattern of consumption. Similarly, each of the changes in the distribution of income brought about by governmental agencies carried with it a change in consumption. In the state of Minnesota alone it has been estimated that 70 millions of dollars a year has been distributed in direct and work relief. Of course this has had an important effect on individual consumption.[1] It has helped to maintain the pattern of consumption of certain groups more nearly as they would have been without the depression. Just what the total effect of the various benefit programs has been is probably impossible to measure accurately, but that they have materially modified consumption patterns cannot be doubted.

In the field of recreation there has come a change that may have a profound long-time effect on American living.[2] In all probability the new emphasis on recreation was well under way before 1930; the extent to which it is a depression phenomenon will be difficult to estimate. Nevertheless, it is clear that work relief funds have been spent in no small measure for tennis courts, golf courses, baseball fields, swimming pools, and similar aids to urban recreation. Work relief funds have likewise been spent for travel and road building in vacation areas. The repercussions of this latter movement are not easy to foretell. The development of the Smoky Mountain National Park, hastened by government depression expenditures, has already resulted in the movement out of the mountains of a number of families that had resided there for many generations. The final effect of opening these mountain areas, with the resulting easy access by automobiles, cannot be foreseen at present. It is certain, however, that material changes in the standard of living of many people will result.

During the depression some new elements and perhaps some

[1] See White, R. Clyde and Mary K. *Research Memorandum on Social Aspects of Relief Policies in the Depression.* (monograph in this series)

[2] See Steiner, Jesse F. *Research Memorandum on Recreation in the Depression.* (monograph in this series)

new chaos were introduced into the field of legal protection of the consumer. The establishment of the NRA interrupted some of the activities of the Federal Trade Commission. In fact for many months there was a general lack of clarity as to the division of field among various government agencies. Some of these agencies were growing so rapidly both in personnel and responsibility that their functions appear to have been inexpertly performed. Whether consumers were definitely given as much protection against misrepresentation during the depression as formerly is a matter that should be thoroughly investigated.

Students of government and public administration have long accepted the axiom that in our highly industrial society the consumer is in need of organized protection. This protection has taken two basic forms: (1) the furnishing of information, and (2) the establishment of certain privileges and prohibitions. The development of protection under this axiom has been slow: certification of weights and measures, inspection for purity of foods and drugs, control of distribution of narcotics, curtailment of misbranding, reduction of secret rebates and monopoly profits, are among the important accomplishments that had been realized before the depression of the '30's.

The public has not always accepted governmental activities in this field with enthusiasm. For example, the Department of Agriculture undertook some years ago to formulate standards of quality for certain foods, particularly canned fruits and vegetables. The movement did not gain great acceptance during the '20's, nor has it even during the depression, because the public failed to insist upon or show any regard for government certification. Perhaps this is not particularly a depression matter, but it would seem of more than passing importance, when incomes are unusually low, that the consumer be relieved as far as practicable from the doctrine of caveat emptor. Continued study of practical standards for consumer goods and of factors which have prevented wider acceptance would seem desirable.

The depression brought nothing new in kind in the governmental desire to protect the consumer, but it did seem to bring a different method of approach. In such major social experiments as the NRA and the AAA the consumer was given official representation at the conference table. History may record that the attempts of the Consumers' Advisory Board and the Consumers' Council have been largely futile, but that is not to say they have been insincere. If they were outmaneuvered by the more experienced and better organized representatives of capital and labor, it is not surprising; perhaps it was inevitable. Experience alone will tell whether any such agencies can be of real service. The information appearing currently in *Consumers' Guide* seems much more pertinent to consumers' needs than when the publication first appeared. Little effort has been made at yet, however, to evaluate the effects on consumption of such dissemination of information.

Quasi-public organizations also were affected by the depression. Labor unions, for example, had been relatively inactive throughout the decade 1919-29. From 1929 to 1932 inclusive they seemed to be unable to take any effective action to curb the depression or to promote employment. With the early signs of returning prosperity, however, they became more active than for many years. While there have been strife and turmoil among the unions themselves, their activity clearly has modified the production and distribution of income. The history of their effect on laborers as consumers is still in the making, but no one can doubt it has a bearing on consumption programs.

Whether the impotence of organized labor from 1929 through 1932 was due merely to a lethargy that had developed during prosperous years, whether it was due to the narrow front on which labor was organized, or whether it was inherent in the depression is not clear. An answer to this question involves an analysis of the causes and relations of cyclical phenomena that is beyond the scope of the present memorandum. It is a matter, however, on which more light must be thrown before the future destiny of the consumer can be forecast or controlled.

One of the interesting phenomena of the early period of recovery has been the emphasis on consumer cooperation. This movement has long been successful in certain parts of Europe, although it appears that new impetus was developed by the depression. In the United States the movement has never amounted to very much until the present decade. It is interesting to note that during adversity, in spite of the paternalistic efforts of the government toward relief, consumers have in numerous instances banded together for self-aid. The extent to which this movement is truly spontaneous or is the work of professional organizers may have a good deal to do with its ultimate success. If it is successful, it may materially influence consumer purchases and thus redirect production, for it is part of the philosophy of consumer cooperation that advertising and sales promotional activities shall be minimized as influences on consumption. A complete study of the depression phenomena must include an evaluation of the consumer cooperative movement.

OTHER INFLUENCES

There are, doubtless, many influences other than changes in income and changes in governmental and other group activities that have modified consumption during the depression. Among these, new inventions and new industries play a prominent part. Closely associated with these is change in taste on the part of consumer groups. This latter has an effect on quality requirements and doubtless there are important repercussions between manufacturers and dealers regarding quality and the taste of the consumers. These and other factors need consideration as possible causes of changes in consumption which are indicated.

Chapter II

Measured Changes in Income and Consumption

COMPLETE coverage of measured changes in income and consumption is beyond the scope of this memorandum. In this chapter there is undertaken only a preliminary review and analysis of some of the important and easily available measurements of income and consumption. These data are used for three purposes, namely:

1. To illustrate the type of material that is available
2. To illustrate the conclusions that may be drawn from such data
3. To suggest some of the imperfections in existing information

This review paves the way for the specific suggestions for further research that are outlined in the following chapter, by pointing out both the excellence and the limitations of recorded data.

It is important, at the outset, to sound a strong word of caution. Many of the data on which studies of the course of this and other depressions are being based are so inadequate in scope and inexact in detail as to be positively misleading. The outstanding need in social-political-economic studies is for better original data. Our development of techniques for analyzing statistical material has proceeded further than for the collection of information at the source. Doubtless it is both easier and more interesting for the individual to experiment with the manipulation of data that come to hand than it is to gather facts from the field. The latter is too expensive to be undertaken on any considerable scale, except for the largest agencies. Such efforts as are made even by these agencies are subject to all the inaccuracies to which a large, undersupervised field force is heir. Moreover, the newer series of data gathered in the recent censuses of trade are beset with the growing pains of uncertain classification. This makes their comparability between years doubtful in the extreme.

No claim is made that the data used in this memorandum are completely accurate. They are suggestive; and in the main they are adequate, perhaps, for the tentative inferences that are drawn. Attention will be called to some of the details of imperfection as the material is presented. Certainly it is to be hoped before another serious depression occurs our collection of important data will be greatly improved.[1]

INCOME

The course of the depression and the measurement of its economic effects are more or less familiar, in general terms, to everyone. Total income produced annually dropped from an index of 100 in 1929 to 48.8 in 1932 and then rose to 65.4 in 1935. A considerable part of this change is merely price phenomena. If the dollar figures are adjusted for changes in the price level the reduction is much less serious, as shown in Table I.

---

[1] Probably the most complete bibliography of material in this general field is the Department of Commerce publication, *Market Research Sources*. This source book is revised every second year. The *Statistical Abstract* and *Survey of Current Business* present the most general and complete compilation of specific data appearing in the field. The Marketing Research and Service Division of the Bureau of Foreign and Domestic Commerce issues a large volume of mimeographed releases, reprints, and compilations. *Consumers' Guide* is the official publication of the Consumers' Counsel of the Agricultural Adjustment Administration. *The Monthly Labor Review* is the official organ of the Bureau of Labor Statistics. Both the Bureau of Labor Statistics and the Bureau of Home Economics in the Department of Agriculture issue reports on specific problems of interest to consumers. These are among the important official sources of information concerning consumption and consumers.

TABLE I

NATIONAL INCOME PRODUCED, IN CURRENT DOLLARS, AND ADJUSTED INDEX
NUMBERS: UNITED STATES, 1929–1935[a]

YEAR	INCOME IN BILLIONS OF CURRENT DOLLARS	INDEX (1929 = 100)	INDEX ADJUSTED FOR CHANGES IN PRICES (1929 = 100)		
			N.I.C.B.[b]	B.L.S.[c]	Brookings
1929	81.0	100.0	100.0	100.0	100.0
1930	67.9	83.8	86.5	85.8	90.0
1931	53.5	66.1	76.7	74.0	79.1
1932	39.5	48.8	63.0	60.6	66.5
1933	41.7	51.5	69.2	67.5	71.5
1934	48.4	59.7	75.3	75.7	73.2
1935	53.0	65.4	79.0	80.7	—

[a] The data on income produced used in this table are taken directly from *National Income in the United States, 1929–1935*. U. S. Department of Commerce, Bureau of Foreign and Domestic Commerce. 1936, P. 22. The current dollar figures are adjusted by three separate indexes, namely: (1) The National Industrial Conference Board index of cost of living which appears regularly in the *Survey of Current Business* (2) the Bureau of Labor Statistics data on cost of living, made into an annual index by averaging two Decembers and the intermediate June weighted double (3) an index computed by the Brookings Institution used for deflating production in current dollars in their study, *Income and Economic Progress*, p. 176, Institute of Economics Pub. No. 68, 1935.

[b] National Industrial Conference Board

[c] Bureau of Labor Statistics

No existing index is really adequate to the purpose of adjusting a time series of dollar incomes to comparable purchasing power or real income. No single index can measure precisely the changes in purchasing power that occur simultaneously, but not identically, throughout a country. The weightings experienced in the actual use of money differ for the geographic sections, for different income levels and cultural groups, for different industrial undertakings, and so on. Perhaps the three indexes used here are as nearly satisfactory as any now available. The Brookings index is more heavily weighted with wholesale prices than are the other two, which are cost-of-living indexes. Consequently it has greater amplitude of movement, which results in keeping the adjusted index of income produced more nearly constant during the depression. Probably the cost-of-living indexes give a better indication of changes in production from the consumers' viewpoint than does the Brookings index.

Even the adjusted figures show a material reduction in income produced. There was some depletion of capital during the period, however, which lessened the reduction in current ability to consume. Income paid out, adjusted for price changes, gives perhaps a better indication of the changes in ability to consume (Table II). The data on this matter are from the same

TABLE II

NATIONAL INCOME PAID OUT, IN CURRENT DOLLARS AND ADJUSTED INDEX
NUMBERS: UNITED STATES, 1929–1935[a]

YEAR	INCOME IN BILLIONS OF CURRENT DOLLARS	INDEX (1929 = 100)	INDEX ADJUSTED FOR CHANGES IN COST OF LIVING (1929 = 100)		
			N.I.C.B.[b]	B.L.S.[c]	BROOKINGS
1929	78.6	100.0	100.0	100.0	100.0
1930	72.9	92.8	97.0	94.9	99.5
1931	61.7	78.5	90.5	87.7	94.0
1932	48.4	61.5	79.5	76.5	92.5
1933	44.9	57.2	76.5	74.9	77.6
1934	50.2	63.8	80.5	80.9	78.0
1935	53.6	68.1	82.2	84.1	—

[a] See footnote a, Table I
[b,c] See footnotes b and c, Table I

source and adjusted in the same way as those on income produced.

When the income paid out is subdivided by types of payment, it appears that the different classes of recipients fared about equally badly in the depression, but that the employees gained slightly over other groups in the early recovery. The figures as summarized by the Department of Commerce are shown in Table III.

These data indicate that the great wage earning classes, constituting together with the farmers perhaps 90 per cent of the total population, had their real income cut to about 75 per cent of the 1929 level in 1933 and that it had risen again to approximately 85 per cent by 1935. This then is the *first* measurement of the limitation of consumption, for income produced and paid out is the first determinant of consumption.

Consumption of Physical Goods:—A decline in the total real income received by the wage earner and other classes of

TABLE III

PERCENTAGE DISTRIBUTION OF NATIONAL INCOME PAID OUT, BY TYPES OF PAYMENT: UNITED STATES, 1929–1935[a]

Types of Payment	1929	1930	1931	1932	1933	1934	1935
Employees[b]	65.5	64.7	64.5	64.0	65.4	66.8	67.3
Dividends, Interest Rents and Royalties	18.6	19.3	19.2	19.5	18.3	17.2	16.5
Entrepreneurial Withdrawals	15.9	16.0	16.3	16.5	16.3	16.0	16.2
Total Income Paid Out	100.0	100.0	100.0	100.0	100.0	100.0	100.0

[a] *National Income in the United States, 1929–1935.* P. 30
[b] Includes all work relief wages

individuals not only limits but changes the character of consumption. Data on the consumption of physical goods indicate the nature of these changes. Objective information is at hand to show some of the changes in consumption patterns during the depression and an analysis of this information is a *second* step in measuring the effect of the depression on consumption. Interpretation of this information must be made with care, of course, if the effects of cyclical and other forces are to be differentiated. Moreover, some of the data are admittedly but estimates. Nevertheless in total they furnish a reasonably clear and accurate picture of what has taken place in some lines of consumption.

From the Census of Retail Distribution it is possible to compare the dollar sales at retail made by various types of outlets. These dollar figures may be adjusted for changes in price and then reduced to relatives of 1929. The data so adjusted are shown in Table IV. They show the approximate changes in physical volume of trade through each type of outlet.

Physical volume of sales appears to have increased in filling stations, remained constant in food stores, and almost constant

TABLE IV

INDEXES SHOWING CHANGES IN PHYSICAL VOLUME OF RETAIL TRADE, BY TYPES OF OUTLETS (ADJUSTED FOR CHANGING PRICE LEVEL): UNITED STATES, 1929, 1933, 1935[a]

(1929 = 100)

TYPES OF OUTLETS	1933	1935
Filling Stations	117	145
Food	98	100
General Merchandise	92	94
Drug	82	85
Apparel	69	86
General (country)	68	58
Lumber and Hardware	45	63
Furniture	40	54

[a] Computed from Table on p. 99—*Retail Distribution*, Preliminary U. S. Summary (Census of American Business 1935). Bureau of Census, October, 1936. Adjustments for price changes were made by using the price index published in the Survey of Current Business that seemed logically related to each type of outlet. Exactness cannot be claimed for these comparisons between the three years: in the first place, there was some difference in the classification of stores used in the three censuses; in the second place, the indexes used are not perfectly designed for the purpose. Nevertheless, the striking differences are believed to be significant.

in general merchandise stores (including urban department stores). Moderate decreases are shown in drug and in apparel stores and marked decreases in the sales of country general stores, hardware stores, lumber yards, and furniture stores. In other words, from these data one might conclude that people in the mass purchased during the depression years more gasoline, the same amount of food, nearly as much apparel and general merchandise, but strikingly less furniture, hardware, and building materials than in 1929.

Various data are available concerning the physical unit sales of specific consumer goods. A few items are shown by way of illustration in Table V.

The National Bureau of Economic Research has reported

changes in the physical output of individual commodities, 1929-1934.[2] These data tend to verify those just presented and they add information concerning other commodities. Some interesting cases are shown in Table VI.

The data in Tables IV, V, and VI come from different sources. Estimates are made at different points in the movement of goods

TABLE V

INDEXES SHOWING CHANGES IN QUANTITIES OF SELECTED CONSUMER GOODS SOLD ANNUALLY: UNITED STATES, 1929–1936[a]

(1929 = 100)

TYPE OF COMMODITY	1930	1931	1932	1933	1934	1935	1936
Electric Refrigerators	183	440	390	490	625	770	—
KWH Electricity (domestic only). . .	112	120	122	122	131	143	158
Gasoline	102	108	100	101	109	116	114
Incandescent Lamps	98	102	99	100	114	122	—
Meat	97	98	96	102	101	84[b]	91[b]
Wheat Flour	101	95	93	95	93	90	92
Cigarettes	100	95	87	94	106	113	122
Butter	100	103	80	79	83	78	76
Electric Flashlights	93	81	77	91	109	120	—
Electric Toasters	80	80	64	63	115	125	—
Radio Tubes	75	77	64	80	80	94	—
Radio Receivers	86	77	59	85	91	107	—
Vacuum Cleaners	75	56	35	43	58	72	90
Passenger Automobiles	65	44	30	30	39	60	69

[a] The data in this table are compiled from various sources and probably they are of different reliability. All of them, however, are believed to be reasonably close estimates. The items are arranged in declining order of 1932 ratios.

[b] Not including government slaughter for distribution to relief clients

from producer to consumer, and different bases are used for classification. Nevertheless, it is perhaps permissible to consider them jointly. Certainly, they seem to tell very much the same story of the character of change in total consumption during the depression. A few points may be made from them with reasonable assurance, although without a careful dissection of the secular trend from the data one must be cautious.

1. The total consumption of foods changed very little during

[2] Bliss, C. A. "Production in Depression and Recovery." New York: National Bureau of Economic Research Bulletin No. 58. November 15 1935

the depression. This is evidenced by the physical sales through food stores, by the physical units of meat, wheat flour, and butter sold, and the physical production of potatoes, fruits and vegetables, and milk.

2. The sales through general merchandise outlets, including urban department stores, remained fairly constant during the

TABLE VI

INDEXES SHOWING CHANGES IN PHYSICAL OUTPUT OF SELECTED COMMODITIES: UNITED STATES, 1929, 1932, 1934[a]
(1929 = 100)

COMMODITY	1932	1934
Rayon	111	173
Potatoes	109	118
Fruits and Vegetables	107	109
Milk	104	100
Silk	89	74
Boots and Shoes	86	97
Cotton Consumption	70	76
Cigars	67	69
Wool Consumption	66	65
Auto Tires	52	69
Wool Carpets and Rugs	38	53

[a] C. A. Bliss. "Production in Depression and Recovery." National Bureau of Economic Research. Bulletin No. 58. November 15 1935

depression. This is in contrast to the trend of sales through country general stores. Perhaps the decrease in the latter is due partially to greater mobility, which has resulted in country people increasing their purchases in city stores. To the extent that this is true, the change is not due directly to the depression. Moreover, this shift of patronage may account in part for the maintained volume of sales by urban department stores.

3. The *use* of automobiles seems not have declined. This is indicated by the sales through filling stations and by the sales of gasoline. The sales of passenger automobiles in physical units, on the other hand, showed a very pronounced decline. This is evidence of the ability of people to use automobiles for a longer

period of years than had previously been the custom. It is interesting to note also that automobile tires showed a marked decline in physical volume of output. This is probably associated with an improvement in quality; another partial explanation may be that it was not necessary to furnish tires as new equipment on as many new automobiles during the depression as previously. Certainly the gasoline figures indicate that motor vehicles went as many miles as previously.[3]

4. There has been an interesting shift in volume of production and consumption of different types of textiles. The output of rayon increased materially. The output of silk decreased somewhat and that of cotton and wool textiles decreased much more strikingly. Part of the reduction in wool consumption is due to the reduction in output of wool carpets and rugs. Undoubtedly a weighted index would show some total reduction in yards of textiles consumed.

5. Another case of change in the relative status of related commodities is found in the fact that cigarettes decreased very little and for a brief period while cigars decreased materially and had not recovered in 1934.

6. The domestic use of electricity showed a considerable increase throughout the period of the depression. Associated with this was the striking increase in the sale of electrical refrigerators and the continued active sale of many other electrical devices for the home. One cannot, of course, attribute this increase to the depression—more likely, it may be said to have occurred despite the depression.

7. Durable consumer goods, such as furniture and automobiles, showed a striking reduction in sales. This reduction, how-

---

[3] Increased use of gasoline probably resulted in part from increased use of trucks and busses, although these changes were partially offset by decreases in use of tractors. The net effect on passenger automobile use is not known. Sales through filling stations were increased in part by a widening of the line of commodities carried.

ever, may have been accompanied by no reduction in use, as is indicated in the case of automobiles by the gasoline consumption figures.

It must be remembered in all this discussion that the concept of total goods sold over a period of time is strictly applicable only to a population which is not changing in numbers or in composition. The total population of the United States increased about six million from 1929 to 1936. Such an increase, equal to about the total population of Australia, cannot be ignored in a discussion or analysis of the sale of consumers' goods during the depression. Moreover, it is possible that consumption patterns were somewhat affected by the changing composition of the population during this period, with respect to such characteristics as age, geographical location, and foreign nativity.[4]

RECREATION[5]

There are many things, other than those offered for sale in retail stores, that enter into the consumer's scale of living. For example, the Committee on Recent Social Trends, estimated the annual expenditure for recreation in 1928-1930 at $10,000,000,000.[6] This is at least 12 per cent of the total income produced in those years and it therefore represents a considerable portion of human welfare.

The largest single item in the ten billion dollar total was automobile touring, three and two-tenths billion dollars. It has

---

[4] Problems relating to these population changes are discussed in several monographs of the present series. See especially the memoranda by: Thompson, Warren S. *Internal Migration in the Depression;* Sanderson, Dwight. *Rural Life in the Depression;* Young, Donald. *Minority Peoples in the Depression;* Stouffer, Samuel A. and Lazarsfeld, Paul F. *The Family in the Depression.*

[5] See Steiner, Jesse F. *Research Memorandum on Recreation in the Depression.* (monograph in this series)

[6] *Recent Social Trends in the United States.* New York: McGraw-Hill Book Co. 1933. II. P. 949. This figure is the total of a series of estimates under a complete classification of recreational activities. Perhaps some of the figures are overestimated, but no better ones have been published.

already been pointed out that gasoline sales were affected but little by the depression. Similarly the number of visitors to national parks suggests that this form of consumption remained relatively high. The data are shown in Table VII.

TABLE VII

MONTHLY AVERAGE NUMBER OF VISITORS AND AUTOMOBILES ARRIVING AT NATIONAL PARKS: 1929–1935[a]

	VISITORS (IN THOUSANDS)	AUTOMOBILES (IN THOUSANDS)
1929	174.0	36.5
1930	177.6	42.8
1931	189.8	45.2
1932	161.4	45.3
1933	157.3	36.1
1934	193.5	45.9
1935	209.3	30.2

[a] Estimates published by the U. S. Department of Commerce. *Survey of Current Business*. 1936 supplement. P. 74

The American Automobile Association estimated that in 1933, at least three billion dollars were spent on automobile touring vacations.[7] Twenty-eight million people, in eight million cars, travelled an average of 3,276 miles in 14 days and spent an average of $7.00 per day. Even allowing for overenthusiasm on the

TABLE VIII

INDEX OF FOREIGN TRAVEL, SHOWING DEPARTURES OF U. S. CITIZENS: 1929–1936 [a]
(1929 = 100)

1929	100	1933	59
1930	105	1934	60
1931	90	1935	64
1932	82	1936[b]	72

[a] *Survey of Current Business. Loc. cit.* Of course, not all foreign travel is properly classed as "recreation"; some of it is strictly for business purposes. Perhaps the travel arising from the two causes has been affected about the same by cyclical forces. "Object of travel" shows less than 10 per cent for business in 1934.

[b] First nine months

[7] This is essentially the estimate used by J. F. Steiner in *Recent Social Trends. Loc. cit.*

part of the AAA, it would seem that the depression did not seriously curtail domestic vacation travel. Perhaps vacation within the United States was maintained during the depression at the expense of foreign travel. This is clearly suggested by Table VIII.

The next largest item in the ten billion dollar estimate is one and a half billion dollars for moving pictures. The estimated weekly attendance at movie theaters during the depression is as follows:[8]

	Millions of Persons
1929	95
1930	110
1931	75
1932	60
1933	60
1934	70
1935	80

These figures show an important reduction, although the totals in the depression years still were the equivalent of an attendance once a fortnight for every man, woman, and child in the population.

During the depression both radio broadcasting and the installed number of receiving sets increased continuously. From 1930 to 1936 the total number of radio sets, exclusive of auto radios, increased steadily from 12 million to nearly 23 million. In addition, auto radios have increased from none in 1930 to 3 million in 1936.[9]

Organized community recreation appears to have increased during the depression. A ten-year review published by the National Recreation Association presents estimates of many im-

---

[8] Mimeographed release of the Department of Commerce. Bureau of Foreign and Domestic Commerce, Marketing Research Division, reprint from "Motion Pictures Abroad."

[9] Data from 1930 U. S. Census of Population and McGraw-Hill radio surveys. New York: McGraw-Hill Book Co. 1936

portant developments between 1925 and 1935; the number of employed people in charge of community recreational activities are reported to have increased from 17,000 to 44,000 in the decade, and the expenditures from $19,000,000 to over $37,000,000.[10] Even the changes reported in facilities and expenditure between 1933 and 1935 are marked:

	1933	1935
Outdoor playgrounds	7,434	9,650
Recreation buildings	777	1,149
Bathing beaches	530	605
Softball diamonds	5,572	7,696
Handball courts	912	1,426
Employed leaders	28,368	43,976
Total expenditures	$27,065,854	$37,472,409

Organized community recreation was increasing during the 1920's, but the policy of paying leaders out of relief funds gave it a decided further impetus during the depression. What will happen when this subsidy is removed is uncertain.

Unemployed groups have organized orchestras, play production groups, gymnasium classes, sketching and painting classes, and similar activities. In part these groups have been furnished leadership and other assistance out of relief funds, while in part they have been spontaneous developments.

There seems also to have been an increase in interest in photography among both employed and unemployed. This has been so decided as to have a considerable effect on the techniques employed. While no statistical evidence is at hand, inspection of exhibits of photography discloses rapid changes in object, perspective, and finish in much of the work both of professionals and of amateurs. Moreover the development of little-camera

---

[10] These data leave much to be desired in the matters of precision and completeness, but the trend they suggest appears to be real. See Steiner, Jesse F. *Research Memorandum on Recreation in the Depression;* White, R. Clyde and Mary K. *Research Memorandum on Social Aspects of Relief Policies in the Depression.* (monographs in this series)

clubs has been almost entirely a depression phenomenon. Probably a similar influence has been exerted in other fields of art. The depression appears to have stimulated many forms of household games. Contract bridge and its variations is a low cost entertainment that has filled many "leisure" hours. Jig-saw puzzles, revival of ping-pong, monopoly, badminton, and many other games requiring a minimum of monetary expenditure have each contributed a little part, perhaps, to relieve the strain of business adversity or the monotony of unemployment. Data are difficult to present in statistical form, but it appears to be certain that many new forms of leisure time activity have entered the consumption patterns of people in all classes.

FAMILY BUDGETS

The study of family cost of living offers another way to measure the effect of the depression on consumers. Two different types of studies are frequently included under this general title, namely, (a) the application of price changes to a fixed pattern or budget of expenditures and (b) the recording of actual purchases and prices. The first type permits an analysis of the relative purchasing power of income at different dates, or the money income necessary under different price conditions to provide a fixed scale of living. The latter type may be used to show changes in the character of consumption that occur from time to time, but does not show directly the cause of the changes. The usefulness of the first type depends in part upon the extent to which the weights used actually apply to the particular income groups that are being studied, while the usefulness of the second type depends in part upon the accompanying analysis of the causes of change in consumption patterns.

There are no studies of either type that are entirely satisfactory for estimating the effect of the depression upon consumption. Cost of living information is generally associated in the public mind with the Bureau of Labor Statistics, but the index published by that Bureau during the early years of the depression was based upon weights that had lost much of their original realism. Moreover, these weights were based on the expenditures of wage earners and low salaried workers only, so they might easily be misleading if applied to other income groups. Recently the Bureau has undertaken a new study of the purchases of employed wage earners and low salaried workers throughout the United States and another study of the cost of living of federal employees living in Washington. Preliminary reports on these studies are appearing, but the lack of time continuity in these studies makes them of minor value for the specific purpose of tracing the course of recent or future cyclical movements.[11]

From 1920 to 1929 the Heller Committee of the Department of Economics, University of California, prepared budgets showing typical spending ways of (1) a wage earner, (2) a clerk, (3) an executive in the San Francisco area. These studies included estimates, based on samples, of the quantity of goods and services which a given standard of living required. Prices were applied to these estimates to give the cost of the standards. From 1927 to 1930, especially, annual changes based on interviews were made in the budgets to eliminate obsolete items and add new ones. Since 1930, however, the weights have been approximately constant so that the total costs reported from year to year represent merely the changes brought about by changes in the general price level and in the relations among specific prices. In spite of these obvious shortcomings, the comparisons made by this committee of the changes in percentage distribution of expenditures that would have been necessary to maintain a

---

[11] See, for example, Williams, Faith M. "Measuring Changes in Cost of Living of Federal Employees." *Monthly Labor Review.* 38:511-517. No. 3. March 1934; and "New Study of Money Disbursements of Wage Earners." *Monthly Labor Review.* 40:861-866. No. 4. April 1935; also Kaplan, A. D. H. "Distribution of Family Income in Urban Communities." *Journal of Marketing.* April 1937

fixed budget of consumption is of interest. Such comparison is given in Table IX.

TABLE IX

CHANGES IN INCOME AND IN PERCENTAGE DISTRIBUTION OF EXPENDITURES[a]
1929-1932

ITEM	EXECUTIVE			CLERK			WAGE-EARNER		
	1929	1932	% change	1929	1932	% change	1929	1932	% change
Food	15.6	13.7	−1.9	32.6	29.6	−3.0	34.7	30.4	−4.3
Clothing.	13.7	10.8	−2.9	17.0	14.6	−2.4	15.4	12.3	−3.1
Shelter	37.8	34.4	−3.4	29.5	30.5	1.0	29.3	32.2	2.9
Miscellaneous . .	32.9	41.1	8.2	20.9	25.3	4.4	20.6	25.1	4.5

[a] Data from Report of the Heller Committee for Research in Social Economics, University of California, Berkeley. January, 1933. (Mimeographed)

These data might erroneously be interpreted to mean that a larger percentage of income actually was reserved for "miscellaneous" expenditures in 1932 than in 1929 while there was a reduction in the percentage used for food, clothing, and shelter, in contradiction of Engel's laws of consumption. All they really mean is that *if* the same things had been purchased in 1932 as in 1929, the changes in relative prices would have caused food to cost a smaller, and "miscellaneous" to cost a larger proportion of the total expenditures. While this is important for some purposes, it does not tell what actually happened to consumption during the depression.

Two studies made at the University of Minnesota have a more direct bearing, perhaps, upon the behavior of consumers during the depression. The first of these compares the income and expenditures of a group of 400 families of students at the University of Minnesota for the years 1929 and 1931; the second makes a similar comparison for a second group of families for the years 1932 and 1934. In each case the group included practically the entire membership of a large freshman class and, consequently, represented both urban and rural families. Approximately 20 per cent of the data were based on family account books while the remainder were estimated, but analysis disclosed no important differences between these two groups. Tables X, XI, and XII summarize the results of the first Minnesota study.[12]

This study emphasizes two points in particular: first, that people do not decrease their expenditures for the ordinary items in their budget until their incomes have been reduced; second,

TABLE X

INDEXES OF 1931 EXPENDITURES PER ADULT UNIT IN GROUPS WHOSE INCOMES DID NOT DECREASE MORE THAN FIVE PER CENT SINCE 1929, BY SIZE OF 1929 INCOME PER ADULT UNIT[a]

(1929 – 100)

	1929 INCOME PER ADULT UNIT					
	0–$559	$560–$824	$825–$1,224	$1,225–$1,849	$1,850–$2,799	$2,800 and over
INCOME	99.5	99.5	100.5	100.0	101.0	97.5
Expenditures						
Food	95	95	91	95	95	100
Clothing	100	97	100	92	100	130
Housing	99	101	100	109	114	99
House operating . . .	96	106	105	100	96	99
Health and education .	106	101	129	115	130	76
Automobile	110	85	96	93	113	125
Recreation	107	104	101	108	110	100
Total	100	100	102	100	107	100
Balance available for investment.	85	95	97	100	85	94

[a] Data from Vaile, R. S. Op. cit. (see note 12 below)

that there is a considerable amount of leeway in certain classes of expenditures—such as those for the operation of automobiles and those for recreation and benevolence—for curtailment of expenditures, while there is comparatively little such opportunity to reduce expenses for housing and house operating. Food and clothing occupy middle ground, the reduction in ex-

[12] Vaile, R. S. *Impact of the Depression on Business Activity and Real Income in Minnesota.* Minneapolis: University of Minnesota Studies in Economics and Business 8. 1933. Pp. 43-48

penditures exceeding only a little the reduction in prices.[13] These conclusions appear to agree closely with those drawn from the Heller study.

The second study at the University of Minnesota was made in February 1935, when an inquiry was made of the families of

TABLE XI

INDEXES OF 1931 EXPENDITURES PER ADULT UNIT IN GROUPS WHOSE INCOMES
DECREASED MORE THAN FIVE PER CENT SINCE 1929, BY SIZE OF 1929
INCOME PER ADULT UNIT[a]
(1929 = 100)

	1929 INCOME PER ADULT UNIT					
	0–$559	$560–$824	$825–$1,224	$1,225–$1,849	$1,850–$2,799	$2,800 and over
INCOME	85	82	75	74	74	70
Expenditures						
Food	91	84	87	85	85	84
Clothing.	90	82	75	78	76	75
Housing	92	100	95	95	99	90
House operating . . .	95	72	84	88	83	83
Health and education .	101	93	78	81	113	71
Automobile	72	66	66	67	43	53
Recreation	84	87	80	70	80	78
Total	91	84	79	80	82	76
Balance available for investment	—[b]	59	60	57	56	61

[a] Data from Vaile, R. S. *Op. cit.* (See note 12, P. 29)
[b] Income was $8.00 less than expenditures

300 university freshmen concerning the changes that had taken place in their income and expenditures, the year 1934 being compared with the year 1932. Of the total number, 57 per cent had suffered a decrease in income and 43 per cent had enjoyed an increase. The following percentage of families with increased income reported that their expenditures had increased in specific ways: (1) payment of debts, 42 per cent; (2) education, recrea-

[13] It is important to keep in mind that a study such as this does not directly reveal changes in the quantity or quality of goods purchased.

tion, and similar expenditures, 48 per cent; (3) purchase of durable goods, such as automobiles, 34 per cent; (4) purchase of food and other necessities, 28 per cent; and (5) purchase of more expensive clothing, 17 per cent.[14]

The families with decreased income reported that they had reduced expenditures as follows: (1) purchase of durable

TABLE XII

REDUCTION IN INCOME AND EXPENDITURES IN 1931, AND PERCENTAGE DISTRIBUTION OF REDUCTION IN EXPENDITURES BY TYPE OF EXPENDITURE, PER ADULT UNIT IN GROUPS WHOSE INCOMES DECREASED MORE THAN FIVE PER CENT SINCE 1929, BY SIZE OF 1929 INCOME PER ADULT UNIT[a]

	1929 Income per Adult Unit					
	0– $559	$560– $824	$825– $1,224	$1,225– $1,849	$1,850– $2,799	$2,800 and over
Reduction in income in 1931 . . .	$59	$121	$260	$400	$566	$1,200
Reduction in expenditures in 1931 .	$38	$99	$170	$231	$286	$556
Percentage of total reduction represented by reducing expenses for:						
Food	23.7	22.7	12.6	11.9	11.1	7.6
Clothing	13.2	11.4	11.9	11.0	12.1	8.5
Housing	15.8	—	4.0	4.2	1.1	7.1
House operating	5.6	25.0	10.6	7.1	12.8	8.5
Health and education	3.0	5.7	20.2	11.3	10.8	17.2
Automobile	20.4	23.8	26.2	21.5	30.8	33.7
Recreation.	18.3	11.4	14.5	33.0	21.3	17.4
Total	100	100	100	100	100	100
Reduction in amount available for investment.	$21	$22	$90	$169	$280	$644

[a] Data from Vaile, R. S. Op. cit. (see note 12, p. 29)

goods, 62 per cent; (2) purchase of clothing, 60 per cent; (3) rent or home upkeep, 40 per cent; (4) education, recreation, and similar expenses, 36 per cent; (5) debt payments, 29 per cent; and (6) purchase of food, 22 per cent.

This second study emphasizes the importance of durable goods and of debts in the changed distribution of income brought about by depression and recovery.

[14] Filipetti, G. and Vaile, R. S. The Economic Effect of the NRA. Minneapolis: University of Minnesota Studies in Economics and Business 11. 1935. Pp. 77-79

Quality of Merchandise.—Changes in quality of merchandise, however, had a considerable influence on consumption patterns. With decreasing incomes there seems to have been a general movement to maintain a scale of living by relinquishing some of the niceties of quality. There was the accompanying tendency on the part of the manufacturers to produce and among retailers to handle products at lower prices, made possible in part by poorer quality. This lowering of quality was especially noticeable in the loading of silks and the reducing of quality of rayons by using cheaper yarns as well as by reducing the count in the weave by stretching.[15]

In the study at the University of Minnesota comparing expenditures in 1931 with those in 1929 it was found that the sales of exclusive and high priced goods had sharply declined, whereas sales of medium and low priced goods in almost all lines were approximately equal to the 1929 figures. For example, exclusive cafes and tea rooms suffered an appreciable loss of patronage and reductions of 12 cents in average check. On the other hand, the medium priced eating places experienced no such decrease in business and only a 3 cent to 4 cent drop in average check. This apparent trading down was typical in practically all lines of retail trade.[16]

This cheapening of quality was not limited to any particular line. There has been jerrybuilding in housing with its counterpart in furniture and home-furnishing. Men's clothing and women's apparel, particularly the latter, have suffered a general decline in quality standards. What effect did all of this have on consumer buying patterns and satisfactions? Among the possible effects, it well may have added to buying resistance, thus creat-

---

[15] Nystrom, P. H. "A Restatement of the Principles of Consumption to Meet Present Conditions." *Journal of Home Economics.* 24:869. October 1932

[16] Vaile, Roland S. *Impact of the Depression on Business Activity and Real Income in Minnesota.* Minneapolis: University of Minnesota Studies in Economics and Business 8. 1933. P. 47

ing a vicious circle. Quality was lowered as a result of depression conditions and consumers bought less because of poor quality, which further aggravated the depression.

It is not certain, however, that the buying habits developed in this circle were entirely to the disadvantage of the consumer. Perhaps the trading down provided an escape from "conspicuous consumption." Quality of merchandise is so complex a thing that consumers who were forced, for example, to buy "poor" ones instead of "good" ones during the depression conceivably may decide to purchase two "poor" ones instead of one "good" one when their purchasing power is restored. Purchases during

TABLE XIII

PERCENTAGE DISTRIBUTION OF RETAIL SALES BY TYPES OF OPERATION:
UNITED STATES, 1929, 1933[a]

TYPE OF OPERATION	PERCENTAGE DISTRIBUTION	
	1929	1933
Independent stores	77.5	71.2
Chain stores	20.0	25.2
All others	2.5	3.6
Total	100.0	100.0

[a] U. S. Bureau of the Census, Retail Distribution, 1929 and 1933. There is an undetermined error in these figures due to change in classification. Probably this does not seriously affect the present comparison. The same comments apply to Table XIV as well.

recovery should be followed closely with a view to finding the extent of change in consumers' ideas of "quality."

It is generally recognized that chain stores sell many types of merchandise at lower prices than do independent stores.[17] That

_____

[17] See, for example, Taylor, M. D. "Prices of Chain and Independent Grocery Stores in Durham, North Carolina." *Harvard Business Review.* 8:413-424. July 1930; Bjorklund, E. and Palmer, J. L. *Study of Prices of Chain and Independent Grocers in Chicago.* University of Chicago Press. 1930; Alexander, R. S. *A Study in Retail Grocery Prices.* New York. *Journal of Commerce.* 1930; Vaile, R. S. and Child, A. M. *Grocery Qualities and Prices.* Minneapolis: University of Minnesota Studies in Economics and Business 7. 1933

consumers tended to take increasing advantage of these lower prices during the depression is indicated by a comparison of sales through different types of retail outlets as reported by the Bureau of the Census for 1929 and 1933 (Table XIII).

This movement toward chain store purchases during the depression is particularly noticeable in certain lines of trade, as indicated by Table XIV. These data are not conclusive, however, for two reasons. The classification and coverage may be

TABLE XIV

SALES IN RETAIL CHAIN STORES AS PERCENTAGES OF TOTAL RETAIL SALES, BY TYPES OF STORES, SHOWING AMOUNT OF INCREASE 1929–1933: UNITED STATES[a]

TYPE OF STORE	1929	1933	INCREASE
All Stores	20.0	25.2	5.2
Combination Grocery and Meats	32.2	43.7	11.5
Cigar Stores	25.1	33.9	8.8
Shoe Stores	38.0	46.2	8.2
Department Stores	16.7	23.9	7.2
Drug Stores	18.5	25.1	6.6

[a] See footnote a, table XIII.

open to question and the data may reflect a secular trend rather than a cyclical effect.

It is sometimes contended that chain stores generally carry lower grade merchandise than do independent stores. If this contention is true, then the money saved through increased patronage at chain stores has been offset in part by reduction in quality. While no complete study of this matter has been made, some light is thrown on it by a study made at the University of Minnesota in 1933 on canned fruits and vegetables. One pertinent quotation is made from the published report of that investigation:

The prices charged in ownership chains are markedly lower, grade for grade, than the prices in other types of retail outlets. The average price of grade A products is 16 per cent lower in ownership chains than in all the stores combined. Ownership chain store prices of grade B and grade

C goods are, respectively, 10 and 20 per cent lower than corresponding prices in all other stores. These lower prices are offset in part by poorer quality. Ownership chain *value,* based on a combination of price and quality figures, is 14 per cent higher for grade A products and nearly 10 per cent higher for all grades combined than the corresponding values in all outlets. This greater value in relation to price is offset by the fact that ownership chain prices are for cash and carry service rather than for credit and delivery service, as is the case with most of the other outlets. . . .[18]

If these findings are typical, and there is no reason to believe they are not, the lower prices found in chain stores are largely a matter of net gain to consumers in exchange for the effort involved in cash-and-carry purchasing rather than at the expense of quality. It will be interesting to see whether consumers will continue their increased patronage of low cost marketing institutions on the return of prosperity.

It is interesting to observe that style, as a somewhat intangible aspect of quality, continued as an active force throughout the depression. "Streamlined" became an almost universal slogan. Guatemala was brought to the United States as a style motif in textiles. While no statistical evidence is at hand, casual perusal of fashion magazines suggests that women's dresses and hats went through style transformations between 1930 and 1936, much as in more prosperous times. Apparently stability of design was acceptable neither to producer nor to consumer during the depression.

New Commodities.—The introduction of new products changes the consumer's buying habits. The automobile is the classical example of a commodity the use of which became so popular in the early part of the twentieth century that the automotive industry was able to pump new life blood into the sluggish veins of industry. Industry in the 1930's is without such a life saver unless it is to be found in the air-conditioning equipment field. To be sure, this is not entirely a product of the de-

[18] Vaile, R. S. and Child, A. M. *Op. cit.* P. 13

pression, but it has been used to create new demand and to stimulate new business during that period. The Department of Commerce did not report new orders for air-conditioning equipment in the Survey of Current Business until 1931, which would indicate that then for the first time sales were large enough to be considered influential. The value of orders booked changed as follows:

1933 ....$ 8,330,000
1934 14,278,000
1935 17,277,000

Changes in tastes also influence buying habits and so do changes in age distribution and in health.[19] However, these changes are taking place slowly and are effective only over long periods of time. They do not reflect so much as other changes the depression period, but they are important enough to warrant study.

Consumer Credit.—One item that influences the consumer's ability to purchase commodities is the expansion or contraction of the use of credit. Brief reference has already been made to the fact that during the depression years more income was paid out than was produced in the United States. Nationally this was possible only with an accompanying depletion of capital, or, at least, a change in its ownership. From the standpoint of individual persons or corporations, however, negative business savings may result from an increase in indebtedness which in turn may have a very direct effect on consumption. Money that is borrowed by corporations or government to meet wage or interest bills becomes available for consumption purchases by its recipients; it is temporarily not available for expenditure by the lender. The increase between 1930 and 1935 in gross public debt, which is referred to in some detail later, amounted to just

---

[19] See Collins, Selwyn D. and Tibbitts, Clark. *Research Memorandum on Social Aspects of Health in the Depression.* (monograph in this series)

over 14 billion dollars or nearly 3 billion dollars per year. This increase in total government debt was underwritten by people with funds available for investment in securities; it made possible a considerable part of the emergency distribution of relief income which, in turn, tended to stabilize consumption of food and clothing during the depression. This somewhat complicated procedure did not directly increase total purchasing power. It did place that power in other hands and in so doing it undoubtedly had an effect on the course of the depression. Further study is necessary to appreciate fully the repercussions of this effect on consumption.

Another phase of the credit situation is found in the changes in consumer credit. The 1933 Census of American Business shows that the percentage of retail sales for which consumer credit was granted decreased from 53 per cent in 1929 to 45 per cent in 1933. Data by types of store are given in Table XV.

The change is somewhat consistent in all types of stores although the reduction in the ratio of credit sales to total sales

TABLE XV

PERCENTAGE OF TOTAL RETAIL SALES FOR WHICH CREDIT WAS GRANTED: UNITED STATES, 1929, 1933[a]

KIND OF BUSINESS	1929	1933
Total	53	45
Grocery and combination stores	49	43
Meat markets	39	32
Department stores	48	42
Variety, 5-and-10, and to-a-dollar stores .	22	16
Women's ready-to-wear specialty stores . .	53	52
Shoe stores	29	26
Motor-vehicle dealers (new and used cars) .	54	46
Filling stations	31	30
Furniture stores	78	74
Hardware stores	50	43
Coal and wood yards	66	57
Drug stores	20	18
Jewelry stores	60	56
All other kinds of business	56	49

[a] *Retail Distribution*: 1933, Vol. I, p. 22 (Census of American Business) U. S. Department of Commerce, Bureau of the Census

was less in women's specialty stores and filling stations than elsewhere.

Annual data on somewhat similar points are given in Table XVI for several types of retail stores. These figures are taken from the Retail Credit Surveys of the United States Department of Commerce. Apparently there was a general tendency for an increase in the proportion of sales done for cash during the depression with some tendency to return to a more liberal credit basis in 1934 and 1935.

TABLE XVI

CASH SALES AS A PERCENTAGE OF TOTAL SALES, FOR SELECTED TYPES OF STORES: UNITED STATES, 1929–1935[a]

YEAR	TYPE OF STORE				
	DEPARTMENT	FURNITURE	JEWELRY	MEN'S CLOTHING	WOMEN'S SPECIALTY
1929	46.5	8.3	26.4	47.9	35.4
1930	46.3	8.2	25.5	46.7	35.6
1931	51.7	10.9	32.0	50.6	37.2
1932	52.9	10.0	34.0	48.7	35.1
1933	51.5	8.8	31.7	44.6	34.1
1934	49.7	9.4	28.5	43.4	35.4
1935	47.8	8.9	27.2	42.2	34.3

[a] From Retail Credit Surveys of the U. S. Department of Commerce

Whether this phenomenon is a result of unwillingness on the part of the consumers to contract debts or of unwillingness on the part of retailers to extend credit is not clear. Perhaps the data presented in Table XVII throw some light on the question, for it is there evident that the percentage of losses from bad debts increased generally during the first years of the depression and decreased again during 1934 and 1935. This experience may have resulted in more stringent restrictions on the granting of credit.

Probably the most prominent field for installment selling is in the automobile business. Data on the percentage of passenger

TABLE XVII

BAD DEBT LOSSES AS A PERCENTAGE OF TOTAL CREDIT SALES FOR SELECTED
TYPES OF STORES BY TYPE OF CREDIT: UNITED STATES, 1929–1935[a]

YEAR	TYPE OF STORE							
	DEPARTMENT		FURNITURE		JEWELRY		MEN'S CLOTHING	WOMEN'S SPECIALTY
	O	I	O	I	O	I	O	O
1929	.4	1.6	.9	3.2	.4	7.5	1.0	.4
1930	.5	2.0	1.8	4.0	.6	8.1	1.2	.5
1931	.8	2.6	1.2	7.0	4.5	7.7	1.6	.7
1932	1.4	4.1	1.5	9.1	1.1	12.8	2.5	1.1
1933	1.1	3.1	2.2	4.8	1.4	8.6	1.8	1.2
1934	.6	1.0	1.4	3.9	.8	4.9	1.3	.7
1935	.4	.7	.9	2.5	1.0	3.6	1.0	.4

[a] From Retail Credit Surveys of U. S. Department of Commerce
O = open credit
I = installment credit

automobile sales made on the installment basis are shown in
Table XVIII. There was a marked reduction of the installment
sales relative to total sales in 1932 both with new and with
used cars. Recovery from this point has come gradually and the
1935 ratio was not quite back to the 1929 figure.

In summary of this point, it may be concluded that public
credit was used to increase the purchasing power of consumers
during the depression, but that the decrease in consumer credit

TABLE XVIII

INSTALLMENT SALES AS A PERCENTAGE OF TOTAL PASSENGER AUTOMOBILE
SALES, FOR NEW AND USED VEHICLES: UNITED STATES, 1929–1935[a]

YEAR	ALL	NEW	USED
1929	64.0	62.6	65.1
1930	63.8	62.3	64.8
1931	61.3	62.8	60.4
1932	48.6	54.6	47.0
1933	56.8	56.8	56.8
1934	56.8	54.6	58.1
1935	61.2	58.2	62.9

[a] Automobile Facts and Figures. National Automobile Chamber of Commerce. 1932 and 1935 editions

tended to restrict purchases for consumption. The net effect of the two opposite movements would be very difficult to estimate, but it might merit further study. Moreover, changes in credit policy doubtless have an effect on the character of consumption as well as on its total, for credit has long been used as an effective device in competitive selling.

Government Expenditures.—The depression has impinged directly upon the consumer, also, in the growing importance of government expenditures. Table XIX shows the importance of these expenditures in the national economy.

TABLE XIX

COMPARISON OF TOTAL GOVERNMENT EXPENDITURES AND NATIONAL INCOME PRODUCED, AND GROSS PUBLIC DEBT: UNITED STATES, 1900, 1910, 1920, 1930–1935

YEAR	NATIONAL INCOME PRODUCED[a] (IN MILLIONS OF DOLLARS)	GOVT. EXPENDITURES[b]		GROSS PUBLIC DEBT[b] (IN MILLIONS OF DOLLARS)
		TOTAL AMOUNT (IN MILLIONS OF DOLLARS)	PERCENTAGE OF NATIONAL INCOME	
1900	16,200	1,492	9.2	3,034
1910	30,100	2,580	8.6	4,859
1920	74,300	11,024	14.8	33,099
1930	67,900	12,373	18.2	33,878
1931	53,500	12,855	24.0	35,486
1932	39,500	13,417	34.0	39,172
1933	41,700	13,478	32.3	42,468
1934	48,400	15,500	32.0	47,226
1935	53,000	14,509	27.4	47,978

[a] Data for 1900, 1910, 1920 from estimates made by the National Industrial Conference Board; for 1930–1935 from *National Income in the United States, 1929–1935.* U. S. Department of Commerce, Bureau of Foreign and Domestic Commerce, 1936

[b] Total for federal, state, and local governments. Data from estimates made by the National Industrial Conference Board

Clearly the changes are not all the result of the depression, but some redirection of income has occurred during depression years. This redirection has been much more evident in some lines than in others. Perhaps the data for Minnesota are representative of the general situation. Expenditures for education and for highways—two very important fields of government activity—decreased materially. A large increase occurred only in expenditures for public welfare—relief employment, direct relief, and so on—which expenditures made possible the uniformity of consumption of foodstuffs and other basic commodities referred to in Table XX.

TABLE XX

GOVERNMENTAL EXPENDITURES BY TYPES OF EXPENDITURES: MINNESOTA, 1931–1935[a]

TYPE OF EXPENDITURE	EXPENDITURES (IN MILLIONS OF DOLLARS)				
	1931	1932	1933	1934	1935
Education[b]	65.3	63.1	53.6	49.6	54.1
Highways[b]	68.6	63.9	38.8	39.7	43.0
Social Security and Public Welfare (incomplete)	13.0	17.9	33.3	87.2	89.5
Other State Expenditures	11.5	11.9	11.4	12.2	13.4
Total	158.4	156.8	137.1	188.7	200.0

[a] Report of the Minnesota State Planning Board. December 1936. Part I, p. 34
[b] Total for federal, state, and local governments

Recognition of the Consumers.—The changes in income and consumption that have occurred since 1929 have been accompanied by an increased recognition of the consumer and his problems. Individuals have been forced to think more of their status as consumers and somewhat less of themselves as producers. Groups of individuals have combined in various self-aid projects. Organized governments have given direct aid to consumers and indirect aid through various protective measures.

The consumer cooperative movement is an important form of self-aid that has developed especially in the latter part of the period; in 1935 retail sales through consumer organizations are reported to have increased 20 per cent while all retail sales increased only 14 per cent. The movement is still small in this country, however, for total sales of all societies in 1933 were only forty million dollars out of total retail sales amounting to over twenty-five billion.

The New Deal administration has been given the reputation of being consumer minded, at least by some of its friendly spokesmen.[20] Emphasis on "purchasing power" of consumers, the electric power "yardstick" of the TVA, the Consumers' Division of the NRA, and the Consumers' Council of AAA are all said to be evidences of direct interest in the consumer.

There appears to be little in the statistical record to show that these efforts have actually benefited consumers directly. The claims of accomplishments of the consumer cooperatives have been attacked with considerable force and apparent realism.[21] The NRA codes clearly failed to give the measure of protection that some had predicted, and since the end of active life of NRA, even the little advantage they might have given has been lost again.

Standardization and improvement in quality in the interest of the consumer appear not to have occurred during the depression as rapidly as earlier. Under NRA some attempt in this direction was intended and about 40 per cent of codes indicated some definite specifications as to quality, quantity, sizes, adulteration, and so on. These provisions, however, represented merely the codification of existing practices and probably made less forward progress than the trade practice conferences of the previous decade.[22]

Attempts were made to pass a more rigid food and drug act in the interest of consumers, but without success. Rather, the Patman bill was passed to protect dealers' margins and manufac-

---

[20] See, for example, Blaisdell, T. C. "The Consumer's Plan and the New Deal." *Journal American Statistical Association*. 30:185-190. No. 189. A Supplement. March 1935

[21] See, for example, Mathews, J. B. "The Cooperatives." *The Atlantic Monthly*. 158:705-715. No. 6. December 1936

[22] See, for example, Thorp, W. L. "Codes and the Consumer." *Journal American Statistical Association*. 30:191-196. No. 189. A Supplement. March 1935

turers' vested interests in particular brands of commodities. Whether this sort of legislation will prove to be in the interest of consumers remains to be seen, but it hardly seems likely.

Previous to the depression of the 1930's, legislation had been designed to protect and favor competition among producers. This was done on the assumption that through competition the consumer is most adequately protected. The New Deal administration is said to have challenged this claim. And yet the first moves of the administration have all been in the direction of restriction of output. Curtailment of volume would seem, generally, to be contrary to consumers' interests. Consequently, it may have been unfortunate for the consumer that the shift was made from the effort to prevent monopoly and fraud to the effort to readjust relative purchasing power through various restrictive devices.

SUMMARY AND CONCLUSION

The foregoing, while in no sense a complete review of all the studies that have been made and that might throw some light on the plight of the consumer, is intended to sample, over a wide area, the existing types of data on the most easily measured movements. It is illustrative, not comprehensive. As this is being written there comes to hand, for example, a bulletin from the National Bureau of Economic Research on the recovery in wages and employment.[23] Moreover, the recent publication of the Bureau of Foreign and Domestic Commerce on the national income 1929-1935 presents information many details of which have not been utilized here.[24] From the data presented the following points may be repeated in summary.

1. Real income produced fell from its 1929 level to an index of 63 in 1932 and increased to 79 in 1935. Real income paid out,

---

[23] Wolman, Leo. *The Recovery in Wages and Employment*. National Bureau of Economic Research Bulletin 63. December 1936

[24] *National Income in the United States, 1929-1935*. U. S. Department of Commerce, Bureau of Foreign and Domestic Commerce. 1936

in contrast, reached its lowest point of 76.5 in 1933 and increased to 82 in 1935. The purchasing power of the wage earning classes reached its low point of 75 in 1933 and had recovered to 85 by 1935.

2. The consumption of specific commodities exhibited marked differences in cyclical fluctuations. Gasoline, domestic electric power, and some other items were used in increased quantities. Total food consumption remained about constant, as did department store sales in general. Durable consumption goods fell greatly in sales, but not necessarily in use.

3. There were marked shifts and apparent total increases in recreational activities throughout the depression as well as during recovery from 1933 to 1936.

4. Studies of family budgets show that when income changes there is greater change in expenditures in some lines than in others. Debts, purchase of durable goods, recreation, and medical care are among the most flexible lines.

5. Government expenditures tended to give different direction to consumption during the depression through its emphasis on leisure time activities.

6. Quality of merchandise was apparently lowered during the depression with no effective effort to establish standard grades in the interest of the consumer.

7. Contraction of consumer credit during the depression tended to increase the reduction in consumption.

8. Various movements in the direct interest of the consumer, such as consumer cooperation and the official advisory councils, have accomplished very little of note. In contrast, legislation such as the Patman Act seems definitely in the interest of the producer.

Chapter III

Problems and Projects

IN CHAPTER I certain basic questions were formulated concerning the effects of cyclical movements on the consumer. These questions were:

1. What has happened during the period?
2. Why did these things occur?
3. Which of them have been advantageous and which disadvantageous?
4. How, if at all, may future movements be controlled?

It was pointed out, further, that each of these questions has an economic, a psychological, and a sociological aspect.

In Chapter II a summary was presented of typical data bearing on these questions. The emphasis of these data is particularly on the economic aspects of the first question. There are two reasons for this, namely, (1) much more information is available in this field than in some of the others and (2) other monographs in this series deal with some of the other aspects and questions.

In example of the second of these points, the effect of the depression on health is the subject of one monograph. Consequently little attention is paid to health in this study, although it is recognized that "the consumer" may be affected by changes in health. Similarly, the social institutions concerned with education, religion, recreation, relief and social welfare are all treated elsewhere.[1] So also are such widely different aspects of individual and social life as crime, the family, and so on. Obvi-

---

[1] See other monographs in this series. Titles are on page ii.

ously each of these items has its bearing on "the consumer," but all of them are considered only incidentally in the present study. As a group, these other studies supply part of the emphasis on the sociological and psychological aspects of the original questions.

The second and fourth of the questions raised at the outset involve the broad causal relationship of cyclical phenomena. Their complete consideration is far beyond the scope of the present monograph. They need to be stated, however, to place the present study in perspective. Moreover, attention is directed specifically to them from time to time.

In this third part is presented a critical discussion of the need for additional information and analysis to complete the consideration of the questions raised, with special emphasis placed on the first one. Consideration is given, also, to possibilities of obtaining the desired information and to methods of interpretation. Not all of the questions discussed are directly related to the depression. However, the depression problem often cannot be understood until more general research has cleared the way.

Research in the field of consumption and the consumer falls naturally into several classes. Much of the basic data can be obtained only through elaborate field studies of the census type. The collection of such original material seems to be obviously a task for government agencies. Considerable advance has been made in this direction in recent years. For example, the Census of Trade was first undertaken on an experimental basis in 1927. Since then it has been made nationwide and has been expanded to include many types of service institutions. The data so compiled give a view of consumption of goods and services that is both more complete and more nearly exact than previously has been possible. As these particular studies become standardized in classification and attain time continuity they will be an invaluable source for analysis of cyclical and other movements in consumption. The studies in cost of living undertaken by the Bureau of Labor Statistics furnish another among the many possible illustrations of broad fact gathering that probably can be undertaken only by a government agency. The newer studies in this field, like those in the trade and service industries, promise to be of great value to future analysis. Continued, painstaking effort in this basic undertaking of gathering information at the source is to be strongly urged on the federal departments and Congress.[2]

In addition to the collection of mass data, many studies in the field of consumption may be based on samples. Such studies often can be undertaken by regional institutions even better than by federal government agencies. Perhaps cooperation might be arranged among regional groups for coordination of the findings; some such cooperative work has long been carried on, for example, between the Department of Agriculture and the state experiment stations. More recently the Departments of Commerce and of Labor have undertaken similar joint efforts.[3]

Each of these three types of studies is illustrated in this sec-

[2] The reporting of mass data, involving collection and tabulation, is still beset with numerous problems. That many people are grappling with these problems is indicated by the fact that in December, 1936, both the American Statistical Association and the American Marketing Association devoted an important part of their respective programs to these matters. See, for example, the following papers:

Williams, F. M. "Methods of Measuring Variations in Family Expenditures." *Journal American Statistical Association.* 32:40-46. No. 197. March 1937; Monroe, Day. "Analyzing Families by Type with Respect to Consumption." *Journal American Statistical Association.* 32:35-39. No. 197. March 1937; Reed, Vergil. "Some Suggested Uses for Census of Business Data." *Journal of Marketing.* P. 310. April 1937. See also Gabler, Werner. "Served to Suit the Taste of the Manufacturer, but Not the Retailer." *Retailing.* P. 2. January 18 1937

[3] That there is active interest in studies on a sampling basis in this general field is indicated, also, by recent publications of the societies concerned with the field. See, for example, Bowley, A. L. "The Application of Sampling to Economic and Sociological Problems." *Journal American Statistical Association.* 31:474-480. No. 195. September 1936; Vernon, Raymond. "Predetermining the Necessary Size of a Sample in Marketing Studies." *Journal of Marketing.* 2:9-12. No. 1. July 1937; and Schoenberg, Erika H. and Parten, Mildred. "Methods and Problems of Sampling Presented by the Urban Study of Consumer Purchases." *Journal American Statistical Association.* 32:311-322. No. 198. June 1937

tion of the present monograph. Some attempt is made, also, to suggest the sort of agency by which each study might be undertaken. The latter question is determined sometimes by the desire for continuity of data or analysis over a period of time, as well as by the magnitude of the undertaking.

1. INCOME

(1a) In the first place there needs to be further clarification of the concept of income. There are many questions that lack clear answers, such, for example, as the following:

(1) At what stage in production and consumption does an item become income?

(2) Which items are most appropriately called "income" and which are more appropriately considered as "expenses"?

(3) Does income change with the change in value of existing inventories either of finished consumer goods or of capital goods?

The National Conference on Wealth and Income, a group composed of representatives from universities, private research organizations, and government research agencies interested in the field of income, is undertaking to clarify these and similar questions regarding income. The work of this conference should be continued and supplemented as rapidly as possible.

It was pointed out in Chapter II that business savings were "negative" from 1930 to 1935 inclusive: for 1932 these "negative" business savings are reported as nearly nine billion dollars or over 22 per cent as large as income produced. This distribution of more income to individuals than was produced by business concerns probably resulted in greater consumption of many types of consumer goods and services than would have resulted otherwise, with a corresponding reduction in direction of purchasing power into capital construction. This hypothesis is supported on the one hand by the Brookings Institution figures on lack of savings among low income families,[4] and on the

---

[4] Leven, M. et al. *America's Capacity to Consume.* Washington, D.C.: Brookings Institution. 1934. Pp. 96, 262

other hand by the well-known facts concerning the severity of the depression in the construction and other heavy industries. It seems probable, in fact, that this distribution of income was made possible, in part, by a depletion of total capital, although this point is not substantiated directly by the data.

Neither of the two concepts of income used by the Department of Commerce is satisfactory as a measure of consumption, nor are the two considered together. "Income paid out" by business concerns may be used for consumption purposes by its recipients, or it may be saved by the individuals. No measure is made, in the data under discussion, of the amount of individual savings. It seems probable that "income paid out" could be made to exceed "income produced"—that is, "negative" business savings could arise—in any of three ways. In the first place, capital inventories might actually be depleted and their value distributed among the claimants, which would leave national wealth reduced. In the second place, ownership of capital inventories might be transferred from business concerns in part payment of employee and other claims, with no direct effect on total capital. Finally, depreciation accounts might be so manipulated that it would appear that more value had been distributed than produced, which method would introduce an aberration into both figures. Perhaps all three of these things have affected the data, but there is no evidence in the published report of their relative importance. Some estimate of the change in the national balance sheet would be necessary to permit an approximation of consumption from the income data as reported, and this the Department has not undertaken. Such an estimate would involve all the pitfalls of changing value of inventories, of course, but it might be an interesting supplement to the data now reported.

In another sense, also, neither of these concepts of income is satisfactory. Each of them measures intermediate stages in the processes of production and consumption. That is, each of them counts as income an estimate of the value of future consumption in terms of present values of money, inventories, and capital goods. In periods of severe fluctuations such measurements of income may differ widely from actual consumption, although in the long run this difference may be unimportant. Even in "normal" times, the durableness of some consumer goods may make these differences important. When a house is built, for example, the two present concepts of income count the sales value or the distributed cost as present income. But if the house is built at a point where next year a railroad will run, necessitating the wrecking of the house, it may be questioned whether any income ever was produced in its building, beyond its one-year use.

It may be suggested, therefore, that a third concept of income be recognized and that efforts be made to estimate both its total amount and its component parts. This concept would make income synonymous with consumer use of goods and services.[5] The total might be arrived at by adding together all final sales of perishable and semi-perishable consumer goods and services, and an allowance for use of durable consumer goods. This total might be compared against the present figure of "income produced" adjusted for changes in total capital inventories. A comparison of this concept of income with the other two should be illuminating in the study of cyclical fluctuations as well as other points. The Department of Commerce would be the national agency, of course, to undertake an estimate of income.

(1b) Closely related to the question of definition is that of measurement of income. The Bureau of Foreign and Domestic Commerce in the publication cited explains in detail the methods by which its estimates are made. Obviously, they say, a quan-

---

[5] The National Resources Committee is now working on some preliminary and partial estimates of this sort. Their work is based on the Study of Consumer Purchases being conducted jointly by the Bureaus of Labor Statistics and Home Economics under the auspices of the National Resources Committee and the Central Statistical Board.

titative analysis of income could not include purely psychic in-come derived from beautiful scenery or from works of art, since no standard of measurement exists for these types of income. The limitations of measurement make it advisable to restrict the estimates to the product of, and compensation for, services which enter into the market place—those for which definite bar-gains and payments in cash or kind are made.

This scheme of measurement has the advantage of being prac-tical but it lacks completeness. Not only does it omit the psychic value of California sunshine in winter, and Colorado mountains or Minnesota lakes in summer, but it omits, also, such tangible things as services of housewives, earnings from odd jobs, and services of owned durable consumers' goods. An exception to the market-place test is made in the case of farm products raised and consumed on the farm. This item is included on the as-sumption, apparently, that it is more nearly an economic activity than is housekeeping—an assumption that may not be popular among women. Perhaps a more impelling reason for its inclu-sion is the opportunistic fact that it is measurable.

If full measure of the effect of cyclical fluctuations on the consumer is desired it is essential that an estimate be included of the changes both in family services and in use of owned durable goods. Such estimates are essential, also, when the income at two periods of time, such as determined census years, are being compared, regardless of cyclical movements. Perhaps the in-crease of the change in hired domestic service furnishes a basis for estimating the first, although introduction of labor-saving household devices would complicate the problem. Similarly, changes in consumption of owned houses (an important item among durable consumer goods) might be estimated from the changes in ratio of rented and owned residences.

Income as measured by the Bureau of Foreign and Domestic Commerce differs from income as measured for purposes of taxation in the handling of realized gains or losses resulting from the sale of assets. When the problem is that of estimating aggregate income the method followed by the Bureau seems appropriate, for it avoids the double counting of income and its capitalization. There is reason to suggest, however, that a fall in the value of capital goods is a reduction from the income that was reported to have been produced in an earlier year. This difficulty suggests, again, the pertinence of the consumption concept of income.

(1c) Measurements of the distribution of income among individuals is perhaps the least satisfactory of any of the attempts to gather original data. The sampling Study of Consumer Purchases being conducted jointly by the Bureau of Labor Statistics and the Bureau of Home Economics, will be very helpful as a check on other methods of estimating this distribution. Even then the data for the lower income groups will be incomplete.[6] Whether the problems of a complete census of income are too great to be overcome is not clear, but certainly further consideration should be given to this matter before the decennial census of 1940. If data were available in the census years, it might be possible to estimate the cyclical changes with reasonable accuracy, through an annual sampling.

Other methods of estimating individual income have been suggested and merit further study. Various agencies have attempted to classify families into income classes on the assumption that total income is correlated with certain definite and readily available expenditures. Home rental, for example, has been cited as an approximate indication of income; so have telephones, make of automobile, subscription to certain magazines, occupation, and so on. Norms have not been established on a satisfactory basis for any of these indexes, nor is it certain that

---

[6] The Health Inventory being conducted at present by the United States Public Health Service will give some valuable information on this point. See also "Total Income Received During the Year 1934 by Gainful Workers." Michigan Census of Population and Unemployment, No. 6. March 1937

they could be. Certainly the estimates would need to be made separately for different geographic regions and for urban versus rural conditions. In spite of the obvious difficulties, however, it seems probable that one or more doctoral theses could be undertaken profitably in the careful investigation of methods in this field. After such investigation, regular estimates of income on some sampling basis might be possible.

(1d) In the study of cyclical fluctuations it is essential, of course, to consider real income as well as monetary income. To this end it is desirable that more and better cost-of-living indexes be devised and maintained. The Bureau of Labor Statistics' new Index of Retail Prices is an effort in this direction. Further work should be done, however, with those items of cost of living not measured by retail prices. Moreover, it would be desirable to have a much greater number of regional indexes and separate indexes for the different individual income levels. A still further improvement would be a more frequent change of weights used in the various cost-of-living indexes. This change is particularly desirable when phenomenon studied is that of short time cyclical movement as contrasted to long time trend in standard of living.

The Bureau of Foreign and Domestic Commerce publishes only one cost-of-living index on a monthly basis.[7] This is computed by the National Industrial Conference Board. It applies to living costs of wage earners' families averaged for a considerable number of cities. In addition the Bureau of Labor Statistics publishes monthly a long list of wholesale prices, and quarterly a cost-of-living index for wage earners for a considerable list of cities both separately and combined. These Bureau of Labor Statistics cost-of-living data were calculated throughout the depression with weights that no longer approximated closely

[7] *Survey of Current Business*. 1936 Supplement. Pp. 11, 15, 154, 155. A detailed description of this index is given in *The Cost of Living in the United States, 1914-1936*. New York: National Industrial Conference Board. 1936. Pp. 13-42

the actual pattern of consumption. At present the Bureau is revising its series of weights through an excellently designed sample study of actual consumption expenditures by individual families. When this undertaking is completed it will be possible to have a much more accurate measurement than at present of the changes in the cost of a fixed scale of consumption. Such indexes as will then be available will permit a close approximation of the extent to which any actual individual wage or income will permit continuation of a scale of consumption, but they will not measure the actual changes in consumption that occur from time to time. However, the problems of revision of weights—as to both time and method—will remain.

A separate geographic index was devised for Minneapolis-St. Paul and is reported semi-annually.[8] The weights for this index were obtained from actual records of all purchases, including rents, of 100 families for one year. Current retail prices are used with these weights to calculate the changes in the index. The construction of similar indexes for different cities and for different income levels is greatly to be desired.

(1e) Further study is necessary of the difference between social income and personal aggrandizement. This is particularly pertinent in view of the claims of Chamberlin and others that conditions of monopolistic competition automatically produce a lower total income than would be the case under ideal competition. This occurs, it is claimed, without any necessary change in the distribution of income between labor, capital, and management, but with a lowering of marginal income for each group.[9]

During the depression many firms curtailed production and

---

[8] Unpublished Ph.D. Thesis by E. A. Gaumnitz, University of Minnesota. Current data published in *The Financial and Investment Review*, University of Minnesota. See also Kozelka, Richard L. *Business Fluctuations in the Northwest.* Bulletin of the Employment Stabilization Research Institute. Minneapolis: University of Minnesota. Vol. 1, No. 4

[9] Chamberlin, Edward. *The Theory of Monopolistic Competition.* Cambridge: Harvard University Press. 1933. Pp. x + 213. See especially Chapter V

threw employees into unemployment in order to reduce to a minimum the losses to capital owners. In this they may have been successful, but their policy of self-protection appears to have resulted in a reduction of total real income for the commonwealth which, in the long run, may have adversely affected the capital owners themselves. Further study of the effect of the attempt to minimize personal losses by restricting output might well be undertaken to determine both the effect on consumers and on the firms practicing the policy.[10]

(1f) Certainly it is desirable to undertake somewhat continuous estimates of that portion of income produced which does not enter into monetary exchange.[11] Some sporadic attempts have been made to estimate the production for family use in agriculture and these estimates have been used in comparing rural and urban incomes. No similar estimate has been made of the income produced by the housewife in the low and moderate income family that could be compared against the expenditure for domestic service on the part of the higher income groups. Moreover, it is impossible from existing data to make a satisfactory time-series comparison of real income over the period when certain industries were becoming commercialized. Such industries include bakeries, laundries, beauty parlors, janitor service in apartments, and many similar ones. The general acceptance of these services into our system of monetary exchange has raised the money cost of living. It should, however, have resulted in an income of another sort through freeing the time of members of the household.

Another somewhat similar influence is found in the increased use of labor-saving devices in homes. Electric sewing machines,

---

[10] Vaile, R. S. "Overhead Costs in Agriculture." *Carver Essays*. Cambridge: Harvard University Press. 1935. Pp. 45-57

[11] This point has, of course, long been recognized by workers in the field of income measurement. See, for example, King, W. I. *The Wealth and Income of the People of the United States*. New York: The Macmillan Co. 1915. Pp. 278. Chapter 5

washing machines, vacuum sweepers, and so forth have permitted housewives to add to the non-monetary income of their families with a minimum of effort. In some cases this may have permitted, in addition, continued employment of the wife in an office or elsewhere, with an accompanying money income. Although these changes in cultural patterns are not entirely cyclical, they need to be described and evaluated; and the attempt should be made to determine their cyclical movement. Moreover, the changes in household tasks have repercussions on child training, education, organized recreation, and, perhaps, on crime.

(1g) The point just made suggests, perhaps, a series of studies in which both monetary income and real income are compared against various ethical scales. In the last analysis it is impossible to measure progress except in terms of ethical values. The price system when allowed free play gives a democratic answer to the question of relative values. When the price system is mixed with both political and monopolistic elements, however, its series of evaluations becomes less democratic. If one accepts democratic decision as the ideal, then the effects of the restraints and privileges that enter into our economic system must be separately interpreted. If, on the other hand, one accepts the ideal of dictation by some superior group, it is essential that the superiority of the particular group in control be critically examined. When a dual system of control including both political and price elements is in operation, it is particularly pertinent to review the production and distribution of income in the light of social values. The changes that come with cyclical fluctuations, and with the attempts to moderate or control the fluctuations, merit realistic ethical appraisal, particularly when the democratic test of behavior based on price is restricted.

Organized governments have long been accustomed to grant special privileges to pressure groups, to redistribute some parts of personal income, and to enforce certain forms of consumption while prohibiting others. The depression brought suggestions for changes in these matters. For example, advocates of subsidized public housing projects for low income families have appeared. Better provision for the aged, expanded recreational facilities furnished at general expense, extension of public education into the adult field, partially subsidized electric power for rural districts, are others of the suggestions for redirection of consumption. Each of these suggestions implies that the people, through their government agencies, will take some purchasing power from those who have it and give it to others in a very specific form. Surely when income is distributed on any basis other than the contribution of the individual to the commonwealth, then the relative merits of different claimants and of different forms of subsidized consumption need most careful consideration. If the political tendencies in this direction that started as emergency measures are to become permanent, a heavy responsibility is placed on government to find new ways of determining social value.

Perhaps a method will be devised some time to measure social income more surely and accurately than the combination of individual willingness and ability to pay a price. As yet, no such device has been developed either in this country or elsewhere. One frequently-heard suggestion involves the use of various attitude scales and tests to indicate what society should undertake in the interest of individual consumers. Psychologists and socioligists have made considerable use of these devices in recent years and seem to be developing techniques of recognized validity for several purposes. Economists, on the other hand, still are skeptical of the possibilities of this method of studying value or the associated concepts of production and income. In part this skepticism results from occasional overenthusiasm and misdirection in the use of the techniques, such as was evidenced by the

John Dewey Society in its study of "Liberalism."[12] In spite of the many difficulties and uncertainties surrounding the use of attitude scales, we have the temerity to suggest careful consideration of them and experimentation with them, both in connection with estimates of income and in other matters to which specific inference is made later.

2. CONSUMPTION

It has already been suggested that in one sense no production takes place until consumption occurs. This concept omits, of course, any idea of those satisfactions that arise entirely from creative activity. It does suggest, however, that a much more intimate approach can be made to the effect of cyclical fluctuations on the consumer through a study of consumption than is possible from a study of income and its distribution. Some of the possible consumption studies are indicated below.

(2a) Some measurement of total consumption of individual commodities was reported in Chapter II. These data showed only the approximate total consumption of all people in the United States. There were indicated some of the changes that took place between 1929 and 1935 not only in total real income but in the importance of specific commodities and activities in the consumption patterns of the nation as a whole. The next step would seem to be a determination of consumption patterns of groups of people classified according to various criteria such, for example, as family income, occupation, nationality, age, and geographical distribution. It would be particularly useful to the sociologist to learn more about differentials in consumption patterns among various minority peoples in the United States.[13] Some work has been done along these lines, but very much more

---

[12] For a popular criticism of this study, see DeVoto, Bernard. "Liberalism Equals N^{nx}." *Harper's Magazine*. May 1937

[13] See Young, Donald. *Research Memorandum on Minority Peoples in the Depression*. (monograph in this series)

is needed before there can be full understanding of the effects of cyclical movements on individual consumers.

In the cost-of-living studies already described little or no effort has been made to change the weights during cyclical fluctuations. For the major purposes of such indexes, constant weights for a considerable time are desirable. Changes should be introduced as the result of semi-permanent modification of consumption resulting from new "state of the arts" and so on, rather than the cyclical phenomena. The study of the latter is important, however, and should be undertaken independently.

One possible technique for such studies is indicated in the information gathered from students and their families at the University of Minnesota, as reported in Chapter II. In these two studies data were gathered on the changes in individual family income between 1929-1931 and 1932-1934. Similarly, changes in consumption were noted by budgetary lines and, in some cases, by specific commodities.

The use of university classes for such a study makes possible the gathering of considerable data at slight cost. There is an admitted bias to the group of families reached in this way and the accuracy of the information will depend on the degree of cooperation between the investigator and the student group. In spite of these obvious shortcomings, a coordinated effort to gather such data continuously from a number of universities might prove very fruitful. Perhaps such an effort might be headed by the research division of the Bureau of Foreign and Domestic Commerce, or by the Association of Collegiate Schools of Business, or by the two jointly.

(2b) As each group is studied, attention needs to be paid not alone to the changes in physical consumption but to the correlation of such changes with changes in individual psychology and in group or community development. For example, the permanence with which consumers will accept the changes in quality of merchandise that came during the depression (see 2g below) is a matter of individual and group attitudes. If properly designed measurements of attitudes towards quality were available they would be an important aid in forecasting changes in demand that accompany cyclical fluctuations. It is unfortunate that no large amount of material exists concerning individual attitudes during the depression. It would be well if some one or several institutions could undertake the collection of a somewhat continuous series of attitude and ability tests that may be continued for a period of years on identical individuals. A start has been made on such a study as a WPA project in a few cities. For example, such a study is under way in the Twin Cities where a considerable number of the clients of the Employment Stabilization Research Institute who were tested in 1932-1933 are being retested in 1936-1937.[14]

An expansion and coordination of the excellent work in this field that has been done by such pioneers as Strong of Stanford, Thurstone of Chicago, Paterson and Anderson of Minnesota might well be undertaken. It appears that sufficient is now known about attitude scales, their use and interpretation, to justify the undertaking of a continuous series that would tend to show the effect of cyclical changes on attitudes of people classified in various ways. Perhaps the same general organization for working through universities as suggested above might be utilized for this purpose. (See 2a above.)

(2c) The real property inventories that were conducted in several large cities in 1934 provided a good deal of information concerning housing conditions. The extent to which families had doubled up during the depression and the extent to which people were living in places unfit for habitation were measured. These studies should be repeated, at least on a sampling basis, during

---

[14] See Paterson, D. G., Darley, J. G. and Elliott, R. M. *Men, Women, and Jobs.* Minneapolis: University of Minnesota Press. 1936

the period of recovery in order to show the rate and sort of change that takes place in housing. This is of particular importance in a study of the consumer because shelter constitutes from 15 to 35 per cent of the total expenditures of individual families.

In order that full interpretation may be made of the effect of housing conditions, correlated studies of delinquency, crime, and health should be undertaken. A limited number of such studies have been made and are under way, but much further work in this field is desirable. This is particularly true because of the emphasis that is being placed on some sort of public subsidy of housing for the low income groups. It would seem wise to have all possible information at hand regarding the effects of improved housing before any major program of this sort is undertaken. Doubtless, it will be necessary to have such evidence before Congress, the state legislatures, or other public boards can be persuaded to make the appropriations that would be required for an adequate public housing program. The question of house ownership and its correlation with personal attitudes and behavior suggests itself as a specific field of study. During the depression "homestead exemptions" from property taxes were introduced in Minnesota and several other states as an encouragement to home ownership. Interest rates below the level offered by commercial agencies were reported to be offered by the federal government for home purchase or repair. At the same time, government subsidy was given to a limited number of public and private limited-dividend housing projects to be occupied under lease. The question may be fairly raised whether both forms of housing should be subsidized or whether aid should be concentrated on one or the other. It may be pointed out again that when people launch a new program of political determination of consumption, every reasonable effort should be made to test the relative merits of alternative programs. In this particular controversy such questions as the use of incidental family labor in the maintenance of housing property may be important. Similarly the effect of home ownership on community activities such as participation in church activities, recreation, education, is important. Stability of residence is probably affected by home ownership, but perhaps mobility is really to be desired. These are but illustrative of the questions that should be answered before depression phenomena are permitted to affect social policy concerning housing.[15]

(2d) In Chapter II it was shown that considerable new emphasis was placed during the depression on recreation and leisure time activities. This emphasis has involved the use both of private and of public funds. In order that continued expansion of expenditure in this direction may be justified, several lines of inquiry should be undertaken. In the first place, the premise that production of other things has reached a stage of efficiency permitting or even enforcing an increase in leisure time needs to be reexamined continuously. In the second place, the effect of the various leisure time activities on individuals' attitudes, aptitudes, and health needs further study on the part of psychologists, doctors, and others. In the third place, the relative merits of spontaneous activities of individuals, families, and groups should be compared with the effects of organized community recreation under official direction. Finally, the development of amateur recreational activities such as dramatics, painting, photography, and so on may have had an important effect on the demand for professional services in these fields. The direction of such repercus-

---

[15] Much has been written in the United States and elsewhere during the depression concerning housing. A few of the important books are listed here by way of illustration: Bauer, Catherine. *Modern Housing*. New York: Houghton-Mifflin Co. 1934. Bemis, Albert F. *The Economics of Shelter*. Cambridge: Massachusetts. Institute of Technology Press. 1934. Editors of Fortune. *Housing America*. New York: Harcourt, Brace and Co. 1932. Wood, Edith E. *Recent Trends in American Housing*. New York: The Macmillan Co. 1931

sions would be important in its effect on (a) the incomes of professionals in the arts and sports, (b) the industries that cater to the arts and sports, and (c) the consumption patterns of the patrons. Here again it would be necessary to correlate the separate studies of the effect on delinquency and crime, on health, and on general attitudes and aptitudes.

(2e) A considerable use of automobile trailers developed during the depression. In part this was a phase of recreation, in part it was a matter of mobility of itinerant labor, and in part a matter of semi-permanent housing of unemployed people with small incomes. These three aspects of trailer use should be studied separately. Some of them may be much more temporary than others and each of them may have a direct effect both on the individuals concerned and on community life. It is possible, of course, that the trailer would have developed even faster if there had been no depression.

There is opportunity in this connection for several regional studies of the scope of Ph.D. theses. They would include analysis of the types of people using trailers, the length of time for which they are used, the effect (if any) on land values and home rentals, the effect on labor supply and its mobility in such a situation as the transient labor in the Pacific Coast fruit sections, and the effect on various municipal problems.

(2f) It was pointed out in Chapter II that credit sales and particularly installment sales were reduced during the early part of the depression. This suggests that they had been widely expanded during the earlier period of prosperity. Close study should be made of the extent to which individuals had obligated their future income before 1930 and the effect of these obligations on other expenditures during the years 1931-1933.

Changes in retail credit policy have an immediate effect on consumption, of course; they may have, also, a causal effect on the course of the depression. Some study has been given to these relationships, notably by Professor Seligman.[16] For true perspective, a thorough review should be made of changes in credit policy from 1926 to 1936 with the specific question in mind whether they contributed in any way to the cyclical movements. Where possible, the consistency of policy among many firms should be tested and the relative success of different policies noted. "Success" in this case might be measured both by sales, which affect consumption directly, and by company profits which affect general business activity directly and consumption indirectly.[17]

(2g) It has also been pointed out that people generally purchased goods of lower quality during the depression than previously. An effort might now be made to measure, through attitude scales, the degree of satisfaction or dissatisfaction occasioned by such merchandise. Information of this type would be valuable in planning production programs in the immediate future. The attempt might also be made to determine the extent to which the reduction in quality originated with the request of the consumer for lower priced goods, as against the desire of the producer to reduce costs. Such information would be of the greatest value to manufacturers and would also be of value to any program of standardization.

The measurement of quality of consumer goods is no easy matter; witness the difficulty that Consumers' Research, Inc., and similar organizations have had in making their statements of quality convincing. With many goods style, or even more intangible factors, are important elements of quality. Nevertheless, it is possible to make some reasonable approximations that can be of real use to consumers.[18] Three types of study might

---

[16] Seligman, E. R. A. *Economics of Installment Selling.* 2 vol. New York: Harper & Bros. 1927

[17] The national credit surveys of the Department of Commerce have made available considerable information in this field that was not previously at hand.

[18] See, for example, the methods used by Vaile, Roland S. and Child, Alice M. *Grocery Qualities and Prices.* Minneapolis: University of Minnesota Press. 1933;

well be made for the various phases of business cycles: measure of the objective factors in quality; relative price movements as an estimate of consumers' evaluation of changes in quality;[19] attitude tests of consumers' reaction to the changes. The findings from the three types of tests would need to be examined together.

Perhaps it is too late to do much with this type of inquiry for the past phases of cyclical movement. A continuing series of studies might well be undertaken, however, beginning with the present, by some federal agency or by some state institution in order that information for the future will be available.

3. SAVINGS

(3a) No measurement was given in Chapter II of the effect of the depression on individual savings, although the difference between income produced and paid out suggested some depletion of total national capital.[20] Some information concerning individual savings is available in the form of savings bank deposits, life insurance sales and premiums, bond and stock holdings, and so on. A complete study of the fluctuations in the volume of private savings would entail a great deal of statistical research. Some work has been done in the field, but additional studies are highly to be desired. Such studies should be undertaken for various income classes to indicate among other things the changes in concentration of capital ownership that occur during cyclical fluctuations. This matter is of importance in itself,

and Phelps, Ethel L. "A Study of Popular Priced White Broadcloth Shirts." *Journal of Home Economics*. November 1935

[19] It is recognized, of course, that scarcity affects relative price as well as does quality.

[20] It will be recalled that in 1932 this difference was nearly 9 billion dollars, or 22 per cent of the income produced. This may have had an important bearing on the course of the depression; certainly it was important in its effect on the consumption of individuals whose income comes from capital ownership. See also Fabricant, Solomon. *Measures of Capital Consumption, 1919-1933*. New York: National Bureau of Economic Research. Bulletin No. 60. June 1936

but perhaps the degree of permanence of the changes is particularly so.

The matter of cyclical fluctuations in capital formation has a decided bearing on other cyclical phenomena. Doubtless it has both direct and indirect effects on consumers. Certainly there is opportunity in this field for several Ph.D. theses in addition to the continuing studies of the National Bureau of Economic Research and of the Brookings Institution.[21]

(3b) So many people of moderate income lost their savings during the depression that it has been suggested that they will never again accumulate the previous volume of savings. On the other hand, the guarantee of bank deposits which developed during the depression may have offset in part the fear and inertia toward personal savings that were occasioned by depression losses. The net effect of these contrasting forces should be measured as thoroughly as possible, both by tests of attitudes toward policies of saving for individuals and by measurements of actual savings by individuals and groups. Attitude measurements on this question of private savings might well be undertaken simultaneously in various parts of the country. Such studies might either be conducted under the direction of one agency or institute, or by separate universities in representative areas. Of course in either case the methods used should permit comparisons and some effort should be made to actually correlate and compare the findings.

Perhaps it may be pointed out that if moderate income families make no personal savings in the future, their dollars will go farther in immediate consumption than has been the case in the past. This, together with the acceptance of public responsibility toward savings for old age and disability, would have a significant bearing on the desirable level of private in-

[21] See Kuznets, Simon. *Gross Capital Formation, 1919-1933.* New York: National Bureau of Economic Research. Bulletin No. 52. November 1934; and Moulton, Harold G. *The Formation of Capital.* Washington: Brookings Institution. 1936

come. The relation of these factors and their effect on people as consumers merits careful consideration.

4. PRODUCERS' ACTIVITIES

(4a) It has been suggested that more should be known concerning the part played by producers in determining the quality of goods. Similarly, more adequate study is to be desired concerning the part played by advertising and sales promotion in the various phases of the cyclical fluctuations. It is sometimes claimed that the increase in total volume of advertising that occurs during prosperity aggravates the business cycle. This assumption should be more thoroughly tested. It is somewhat doubtful whether a complete study of the question can be made unless or until the private records of a large number of firms can be made available for analysis.

One possible method of analyzing the relations between advertising and business cycles is described in a study published in the *Harvard Business Review*.[22] This study was limited to the immediate postwar depression; it was limited also in the number of firms included and to the fluctuations in magazine advertising. Similar studies might well be undertaken for the period since then, but data for more firms should be sought and a broader index of advertising should be used if possible. Perhaps the cooperation of the association of national advertisers could be arranged for such a study under the general direction of the Department of Commerce or some university Bureau of Business Research.

(4b) Study of changes in the types of merchandising institutions during depressions might show some interesting effects on consumers' interests. The extensive chain store inquiry of the Federal Trade Commission disclosed many of the advantages

---

[22] Vaile, Roland S. "The Use of Advertising During Depressions." *Harvard Business Review*. 5:323-330. No. 3. April 1927. See also Crum, W. L. *Advertising Fluctuations*. Chicago and New York: A. W. Shaw Co. 1927

and disadvantages of this system in respect to prices, quality of merchandise, service features, and so on.[23] Continued study of the changes in these matters that occurred later and their relation to consumers' satisfaction is suggested. Frequent local study of relative prices charged in various types of outlets, and of the change in price spreads during the course of cyclical fluctuations would be valuable.[24] The Census of Distribution, in its various forms and elaborations, makes available an important new body of information that is helpful in the study of these points.

In this same connection, adequate cost and efficiency studies are desirable in all the fields of merchandising to throw light upon the possibilities of advantage accruing to consumers through cooperatives or other new merchandising institutions. Such studies should be compared, of course, with the actual performance of those consumer cooperatives that were instituted during the depression. The effect of reductions in sales promotion, implied in the cooperative movement, would relate this study to those already suggested on advertising. The attitude of people of all classes toward cooperatives might be tested in the different phases of cyclical fluctuations as an indication of the chances for continued development of the movement. Perhaps there is sufficient history of cooperation in America already to warrant some forecasts; certainly such history should be brought together and analyzed for its relation to business cycles.

(4c) It would be desirable to determine whether changes in consumer insistence upon specific brands of merchandise occurred during the depression. Such changes, if any, might have been associated with changes either in manufacturers' price policies or in quality characteristics. Moreover, they might have had a bearing on the degree of monopolistic competition in some in-

---

[23] *Chain Store Inquiry.* Washington: Federal Trade Commission. 1932

[24] The problem of quality measurement complicates these comparisons, but does not completely prevent them.

dustries, which, in turn, would affect the real income of consumers. The original information needed for a study of these questions would include data on sales of branded merchandise, and tests of consumer attitudes toward brands. Such information might be collected on a sampling basis with the aid of university students in the manner previously described.

5. GOVERNMENT ACTIVITY

(5a) Probably most of the change in government activity following 1929 that had direct effect on the consumer was caused by, rather than a cause of, the depression. Nevertheless, since industrial fluctuations appear so definitely to be matters of multiple causation, consideration must be given to the part played by government in their course. Some analysis has already been undertaken of the effect of the NRA, the AAA, and other mid-depression legislation on at least certain groups of consumers.[25] Further analysis that would tend to show not only the direct effect on these groups but the indirect effect on other groups is clearly needed.

Perhaps some special attention might be given by students of political science and others to the organization of consumers' counsels that would effectively represent consumers' interests in political bargaining. If cyclical movements are to be accompanied, as in the present case, by modifying legislation, careful study should be given to the effects of such legislation on the real income of various social groups.

(5b) Moreover, studies should be started at once on the effect of the Patman Act and the resale price maintenance clause on consumers. The clause appears to give recognition to the proposition that good-will and product differentiation established by

---

[25] Notable in this connection are the studies of the Brookings Institution. See, for example, Lyon, L. S. *et al. The National Recovery Administration*. Washington, D.C. 1935. Nourse, E. G. *Marketing Agreements under the AAA*. Washington, D.C. 1935; and a series of studies concerning the AAA and specific farm products.

manufacturers merits protection against that established by merchants. The extent to which such a proposition may lead to monopoly to the disadvantage of the consumer is at present unknown. That it will lead directly to an increase in monopolistic competition, and thereby to a decrease in total well-being, seems probable.

(5c) Further study needs to be made of the possibilities connected with standardization and certification of consumer goods as a government activity. The early attempts in this field involved merely the setting of minimum standards, which were not always set in terms that were truly applicable to consumer requirements. It appears that little progress was made in this direction during the depression. Such inquiry would involve study of commodity characteristics in terms of consumer desires, the possibility of certifying quality with respect to these characteristics, and the practicability of having goods manufactured according to the established specifications.

(5d) The power of taxation was used during the depression to modify both the institutions serving consumers and the distribution of real income among individuals. Changes in income tax rates, the levying of sales taxes, the partial exemption of homesteads from taxation, the imposition of chain store taxes, all directly affected individual income. The effects impinged with different force upon different social groups. The first step in the study of these effects would be a complete compilation of the changes that were imposed. It would then be possible to analyze the probable results of each change. This complicated field would seem to lend itself to study by a considerable number of individual research workers.

CONCLUSION

In this discussion of the problems of the consumer during cyclical fluctuations, there is admittedly a mixing of several things. It has been assumed that the purpose of each of the suggested studies will be to throw some light on what has happened in order that some corrective devices may be undertaken in the future. In part, the studies suggested involve merely the gathering of historical data; in part, they consider cause and effect relationships; and in part, they suggest the testing of alleviating devices. The principal hope is that they may suggest some fruitful lines of immediate inquiry.

The types of inquiry that are suggested involve several important research techniques. Some of the studies are concerned with mass data and would best be conducted by large, centralized agencies; some would need to be based on samples and could be undertaken by regional institutions, with provision for comparison and coordination of the findings; some of them could be undertaken successfully by individual workers.

It seems probable, for example, that the measurement of income in terms of consumption (1a, above) should be undertaken by the Department of Commerce. Many of the data needed for this aggregate measurement are already collected by the Department, and the gaps probably could be filled there more easily than elsewhere. Similarly, if any census of incomes is undertaken it should be done by the Bureau of the Census (1c, above). In fact, the collection of all primary mass data would appear to be a federal function. If the central agencies operate efficiently in the collection of such data, then other analysts can study and interpret developments without the necessity of contacting original sources. Parenthetically, it may be remarked that this would be a great relief both to the analyst and to the source.

In the case of sample studies, the advantage of centralization is less clear. Regional cost-of-living studies for any income group might well be undertaken by regional institutions, particularly if the actual-purchase method is employed. The problem of measuring the cost of living may be subdivided in so many ways in addition to the regional classification that portions of it may be undertaken advantageously by individual workers (1d, above). Unless, or until the federal agencies complete the process of developing cost-of-living weights to be used both by regions and by income levels, there is excellent opportunity for individual monographs dealing with limited classes. In any such individual studies importance would attach to the reasonableness and importance of the classification used, the representativeness of the sample, and the opportunity for comparison with other studies.

The study of savings (3a, above) might involve some additions to the present collection of mass data by the Department of Commerce. In addition, however, there would be an opportunity for more intimate study of habits of savings by regions, by income classes, and by other criteria. These studies could be supplemented further by measurements of attitudes toward savings (3b, above). These latter studies might well be undertaken by individual workers. In fact, the attitude studies that are suggested in connection with several of the desirable lines of investigation lend themselves well to individual study. (See particularly 2b.) So, perhaps, do the studies of advertising fluctuations (4a), merchandising institutions (4b), housing (2c), and some of the others. Certainly the theory and effect of monopolistic competition (1e), the effects of changing cultural patterns (1f), the ethical evaluations (1g), and the effects of governmental activities (5a, b), merit separate attention of many individuals, for there can be no completely objective testing of these things.

Many of the things that happen during a depression or a recovery are transitory—almost ephemeral—and quickly forgotten. They should be recorded and given preliminary analysis currently. Only in that way can the perspective that comes later furnish a reflection of the highlights and the sombre tones of which the life of a people is composed.

Some Bibliographical Suggestions

ADAMS, M. "On the Trail of the Elusive Consumer." *N Y Times* O '35

ANDREWS, B. *Economics of the Household.* New York: Macmillan. Rev ed. '35

Annual Report of the Commissioner of Internal Revenue. Washington, D.C.: U S Treas Dept Je 30 '35

ARNOLD, J. "Volume and Slackening Growth of Consumption in the United States." *Annalist* Ja 27 '33

ARTHUR, H. "Costs, Prices, and the Consumer." *J Am Statis Assn* Mr '35

Automobile Facts and Figures. New York: Automobile Manufacturers' Assn

BADER, L. "Can We Find Out How the American Income Is Spent?" *J Am Statis Assn* S '31

———. "The American Family Income." *J Am Statis Assn* S '33

BARBOUR, P. "The Downward Offset in the Trend of World Commodity Consumption." *Annalist* O 21 '32

BAUER, C. *Modern Housing.* Boston: Houghton-Mifflin. '34

BEMIS, ALBERT F. *The Economics of Shelter.* Cambridge: Massachusetts Institute of Technology Press. '34

BLAISDELL, T. C. "Consumers' Place in the Organization of the New Deal." *J Am Statis Assn* Mr '35

BORSODI, R. *The Flight from the City.* New York: Harper. '33

BRINDZE, R. "Consumer Cooperatives." *Cur Hist* Je '36

———. *How to Spend Money.* New York: Vanguard Press. '35

BURNS, C. D. *Leisure in the Modern World.* New York: Century. '32

BUSH, ADA L. *Consumer Use of Selected Goods and Services by Income Classes.* U S Dept Com, Bur For & Dom Com. Market Res Series

BYE, R. T. and BLODGETT, R. H. *Getting and Earning.* New York: F. S. Crofts. '37

CARVER, T. N. "Theory of the Shortened Working Week." *Am Econ R* S '36

CARVER, T. N. *et al. Textile Problems for the Consumer*. New York: Macmillan '35

Chain Store Inquiry. Federal Trade Commission. '32

CHANDLER, A. E. *Distribution of Expenditures and a Cost of Living Index for a Professional Group.* Columbus: Ohio State Univ, Bur Bus Res S '32

CHAPIN, R. C. "Influence of Income on Standards of Life." *Am J Soc* 14 Mr '09

CHASE, S. *Economy of Abundance*. New York: Macmillan '34

————. *The Promise of Power.* New York: Day. '33

CLARK, L. *Financing the Consumer.* New York: Harper. '30

COLES, J. V. *Standardization of Consumers' Goods.* New York: Ronald '32

"Consumers Organize Local Groups for Better Quality, Lower Prices." *Ind Standardization & Commercial Standards Monthly* N '35

"Cooperation-Stability of Cooperative Movement During the Depression." *Monthly Labor R* Mr '33

"Cooperative Housing Pulls Through." *Consumer' Coop* S '36

CORBETT, I. "The Activities of Consumers' Organizations." *Law & Contempt Problems* D '33

Cost of Living in the United States, 1914-1936. New York: National Industrial Conference Board. '36

Cost of Living Studies. Berkeley: Univ of Calif, Heller Comm for Res in Soc Econ

A Descriptive Bibliography of American Standards of Living. Am Home Econ Assn, Family Section '34

DONHAM, S. A. *Spending the Family Income.* Boston: Little, Brown, Rev ed. '33

DOUGLAS, P. H. "Place of the Consumer in the New Industrial Set-up." *J Home Econ* O '34

DUBLIN, L. I. "Population Changes and Consumption." *Taylor Society Bul* O '32

DUBLIN, L. I. and BERRIDGE, W. A. *Need for New Surveys of Family Budgets and Buying Habits.* New York: Metropolitan Life Ins Bul '31

ELIOT, T. "Changing Home Standards under the New Deal." *J Home Econ* My '34

ENGLE, N. "Housing Conditions in America." *J Am Statis Assn* Mr '35

ENJEIAN, C. M. "How We Managed." *Survey* S '34

EZEKIEL, M. *$2500 a Year: From Scarcity to Abundance.* New York: Harcourt, Brace. '36

FABRICANT, S. *Measures of Capital Consumption, 1919-1933.* New York: Nat Bur Econ Res Bul 60. Je '36

FILIPETTI, G. and VAILE, R. *Economic Effects of the NRA.* Minneapolis: Univ of Minnesota, Studies in Econ and Bus 11 Jl '35

FOREMAN, C. and ROSS, M. *Consumer Seeks a Way.* New York: Norton. '35

FORTUNE EDITORS. *Housing America.* New York: Harcourt, Brace. '32

FOSTER, L. R. *State Regulation of Installment Selling and Financing.* Newton, Mass: Pollack Foundation for Econ Res. Pamphlet 30. '35

FOWLER, B. *Consumer Cooperation in America.* New York: Vanguard. '36

————. "The New Deal Ahead: The Future of Consumer Cooperation." *Forum* Ag '35

FREUNDLICH, E. "Cooperative Movement in the Present World Order." *Ann Am Acad* Jl '35

FRIEND, M. R. *Earning and Spending the Family Income.* New York: Appleton-Century. Rev ed. '35

FROMAN, L. "Cost of Installment Buying." *Harvard Bus R* Ja '33

GOLDMAN, J. *Prosperity and Consumer Credit.* New York: Harper. '30

GREENWOOD, E. *Spenders All.* New York: Appleton-Century. '35

GRETHER, E. T. "Resale Price Maintenance and the Consumer." *Am Marketing J* Jl '35

GUILFORD, E. "Adjusting Family Spending to Meet Reduced Incomes." *J. Home Econ* N '32

HAIG, R. and SHOUP, C. *The Sales Tax in the American States.* New York: Columbia Univ Press. '34

HINRICHS, A. "Planning, Consumption, and the Standard of Living." *Plan Age* O '35

HOYT, E. "Tariffs and the Consumer." *J Home Econ* F '34

"Influence of the Depression on the Expenditures of Business Women." *Monthly Labor R* D '33

Interim Report of Plans for a Study of Consumer Purchases. Washington, D.C.: National Resources Comm, Consumption Res Staff, Indus Section Ja 13 '36

KALLET, A. *Counterfeit.* New York: Vanguard. '35

KALLET, A. and SCHLINK, F. *100,000,000 Guinea Pigs.* New York: Vanguard. '32

KAPLAN, A. D. H. "Distribution of Family Income in Urban Communities." *J Marketing* Ap '37

KEEZER, D. "Consumer under NRA." *Ann Am Acad* Mr '34

KNEELAND, H. et al. "Plans for a Study of the Consumption of Goods and Services by American Families." *J Am Statis Assn* Mr '36

KNUZNETS, S. *Gross Capital Formation, 1919-1933.* New York: Nat Bur Econ Res Bul 52. N '34

KYRK, H. *Economic Problems of the Family.* New York: Harper. '33

————. "The Government and the Consumer." *J Home Econ* Ap '35

LA CROSSE, H. T. *Consumer Debt Study.* Washington, D.C.: U S Dept Com, Bur For & Dom Com. Market Res Series Mr '35

LAMB, B. *Government and the Consumer.* National League of Women Voters. '35

The Leisure Hours of 5,000 People: A Report of a Study of Leisure Time Activities and Desires. New York: Nat Recreation Assn. '34

LEVEN, M. et al. *America's Capacity to Consume.* Washington: Brookings Institution. '34

LOEB, Harold and others. *The Chart of Plenty.* New York: Viking. '35

LOGAN, J. A. "Does Large Scale Merchandising Benefit Consumers?" *Am Marketing* J J '36

LOUGH, W. H. *High-Level Consumption.* New York: McGraw-Hill. '35

————. "Some Impending Changes in Consumer Demand." *Am Marketing* J Ja '35

LYND, R. S. "Will Grade Marks Kill Trade Marks?" *Adv & Sell* D 6 '34

————. "Family Members as Consumers." *Ann Am Acad* Mr '32

————. "New Deal Consumers: A Study at Close Range." *Ptr Ink* Mr 22 '34

LYND, R. S. and H. M. *Middletown in Transition.* New York: Harcourt, Brace. '37

LYON, L. S. et al. *The NRA: An Analysis and an Appraisal.* Washington: Brookings Institution. '35

MCNIECE, T. M. *Consumers' Rate of Replacement: A Study of Demand.* Report of the 1932 Boston Conference on Retail Distribution. Boston Chamber of Commerce, Retail Board

MARTIN, E. S. "Cooperation." *Harpers Mag* O '34

MATHEWS, J. B. "The Cooperatives." *Atlantic* D '36

"Measuring Consumption Habits." Editorial. *Plan Age* O '35

MEQUET, G. "Possibilities of International Action in Regard to Workers' Spare Time." *Int Labour R* N '34

"Money Disbursement of Wage Earners and Clerical Workers in Eleven New Hampshire Communities." *Monthly Labor R.* Mr '36

MONROE, Day. "Analyzing Families by Type with Respect to Consumption." *J Am Statis Assn* Mr '37

MOULTON, H. G. *Formation of Capital.* Washington: Brookings Institution. '35

———. *Income and Economic Progress.* Washington: Brookings Institution '35

NATHAN, R. "National Income Increased by 5 Billion Dollars in 1934." *Survey Cur Bus* Ag '35

National Income in the United States, 1929-1935. Washington, D.C.: U S Dept Com, Bur For & Dom Com '36

"New Developments in Fabricated Housing Field." *Am Builder* N '35

NYSTROM, P. H. "The Disintegration of Quality Standards in Consumer Goods." *Adv & Sell* Je 8 '33

———. "The Cause of the Present Decline in Quality." *Adv & Sell* Je 22 '33

———. "A Restatement of the Principles of Consumption to Meet Present Conditions." *J Home Econ* O '32

"Obstacles in the Sales Terrain: Fair Trade Laws, Chain Taxes, Retail and General Sales Taxes." With map. *Business Week* O 12 '33

PACK, A. N. *Challenge of Leisure.* New York: Macmillan. '34

PHELPS, E. and GORHAM, E. "A Study of Popular Priced White Broadcloth Shirts." *J Home Econ* N '35

PITKIN, W. *The Consumer.* New York: McGraw-Hill. '32

———. *Lets Get What We Want.* New York: Simon & Schuster. '35

"Post-Depression Purchases." *Fortune* Jl '35

President's Research Committee on Social Trends. *Recent Social Trends in the United States.* New York: McGraw-Hill. '33

PRICE, R. "The Forgotten Consumer." *Bus Ed World.* Mr '34

"Public Services vs Taxation." *Fortune* Jl '35

Real Property Inventory. CWA Project. Washington, D.C.: U S Dept Com, Bur For & Dom Com '34

REED, V. "Some Suggested Uses for Census of Business Data." *J Marketing* Ap '37

Retail Credit Survey. Dom Com Series. Washington, D.C.: U S Dept Com, Bur For & Dom Com '30-'35

Retail Distribution. (Census of Am Bus). U S Dept Com, Bur Cens '29, '33

SADD, V. and WILLIAMS, R. T. *Causes of Bankruptcies among Consumers.* Washington, D.C.: U S Dept Com, Bur For & Dom Com '33

Salaries and Cost of Living in Universities, 1913-1932. Columbus: Ohio State Univ, Bur Bus Res '32

SERDMAN, F. "What Price Furniture?" *Furniture Index* Je '36

Standards of Living: A Compilation of Budgetary Studies. Bur Applied Econ Bul 7 Pt 2 '32

STARCH, D. *Faith, Fear, and Fortunes.* New York: R. R. Smith. '34

STINE, O. C. "Changes in the Aggregate Volume and Distribution of Purchasing Power During Recovery." *J Farm Econ* My '35

STONE, J. F., JR. *Compulsory Spending.* Washington, D.C.: Ransdell, Inc. '34

STUBBINGS, G. "Consumption Analysis: Use of Statistical Diagrams." *Elec R* (Lond) S 6 '35

TAYLOR, M. D. "A Study of Weights in Chain and Independent Grocery Stores in Durham, North Carolina." *Harvard Business R* Jl '31

————. "Prices of Branded Grocery Commodities During the Depression." *Harvard Business R* Jl '34

TEBBUTT, A. *Behavior of Consumption in Business Depression.* Cambridge: Harvard Univ, Bus Res Studies '33

THOMPSON, H. and DOWLING, A. "Trends in Consumer Buying of Household Fabrics." *J Home Econ* Je '35

THORP, W. "Codes and the Consumer." *J Am Statis Assn* Mr '35

TOSDAL, H. "Recent Changes in the Marketing of Consumer Goods." *Harvard Business R* Ja '33

TUGWELL, R. G. and HILL, H. *Our Economic Society and Its Problems: A Study of American Levels of Living and How to Improve Them.* New York: Harcourt, Brace. '34

"The Ultimate Consumer: A Study in Economic Illiteracy." *Ann Am Acad* My '34. (This entire number is devoted to the general topic, with some twenty articles on special phases of it.)

VAILE, R. S. *Impact of the Depression on Business Activity and Real Income in Minnesota.* Minneapolis: Univ. of Minnesota, Studies in Econ & Bus 8 Ag '33

VAILE, R. S. and CHILD, A. M. *Grocery Qualities and Prices.* Minneapolis: Univ of Minnesota, Studies in Econ & Bus 7 Ap '33

WAITE, W. "Some Developments in Technique of Studying Consumer Demand." *J Am Statis Assn* sup '30

WALKER, MABEL. *Where the Sales Tax Falls.* New York: General Welfare Tax League. '34

WARBURTON, C. "How the National Income Was Spent, 1919-1929." *J Am Statis Assn* Mr '35

WEAVER, H. "The Use of Statistics in the Study of Consumer Demand." *J Am Statis Assn* Mr '35

WERNETTE, P. "Grade Labeling vs Descriptive Labeling." *Nat Marketing R* Fall '35

"When Consumers Get Together." *Consumers' Guide* Je 24 '35

WILLIAMS, A. "Standards of Living and Government Responsibility." *Ann Am Acad* N '34

WILLIAMS, F. "Food Consumption at Different Economic Levels." *Monthly Labor R* Ap '36

―――. "Levels of Living vs Standard of Living." *Plan Age* O '35

―――. "Measuring Changes in Cost of Living of Federal Employees." *Monthly Labor R* Mr '34

―――. "Methods of Measuring Variations in Family Expenditures." *J Am Statis Assn* Mr '37

―――. "New Study of Money Disbursements of Wage Earners." *Monthly Labor R* Ap '35

WILLIAMS, F. *et al.* "Changes in Cost of Living of Federal Employees in the District of Columbia from 1928 to 1933." *Monthly Labor R* Jl '34

WILLIAMS, F. and ZIMMERMAN, C. *Studies of Family Living in the U. S. and Other Countries: An Analysis of Material and Method.* Washington, D.C.: U S Dept Com, Office of Information. Misc Pub 223. D '35

WILLOUGHBY, R. "Stalking the Fickle Consumer." *Nation's Business* S '32

WOOD, E. *Recent Trends in American Housing.* New York: Macmillan. '31

World Economic Review. Washington, D.C.: U S Dept Com, Bur For & Dom Com '35

ZWEIG, F. *The Economics of Consumers' Credit.* London: King. '34

Index

Studies in the Social Aspects
of the Depression

AN ARNO PRESS/NEW YORK TIMES COLLECTION

Chapin, F. Stuart and Stuart A. Queen.
Research Memorandum on Social Work in the Depression. 1937.

Collins, Selwyn D. and Clark Tibbitts.
Research Memorandum on Social Aspects of Health in the Depression. 1937.

The Educational Policies Commission.
Research Memorandum on Education in the Depression. 1937.

Kincheloe, Samuel C.
Research Memorandum on Religion in the Depression. 1937.

Sanderson, Dwight.
Research Memorandum on Rural Life in the Depression. 1937.

Sellin, Thorsten.
Research Memorandum on Crime in the Depression. 1937.

Steiner, Jesse F.
Research Memorandum on Recreation in the Depression. 1937.

Stouffer, Samuel A. and Paul F. Lazarsfeld.
Research Memorandum on the Family in the Depression. 1937.

Thompson, Warren S.
Research Memorandum on Internal Migration in the Depression. 1937.

Vaile, Roland S.
Research Memorandum on Social Aspects of Consumption in the Depression. 1937.

Waples, Douglas.
Research Memorandum on Social Aspects of Reading in the Depression. 1937.

White, R. Clyde and Mary K. White.
Research Memorandum on Social Aspects of Relief Policies in the Depression. 1937.

Young, Donald.
Research Memorandum on Minority Peoples in the Depression. 1937.